Modern Mandarin Chinese

Modern Mandarin Chinese is a two-year undergraduate course for students with no prior background in Chinese study. Designed to build a strong foundation in both the spoken and written language, it develops all the basic skills such as pronunciation, character writing, word use, and structures, while placing a strong emphasis on the development of communication skills.

Each level of the course consists of a textbook and workbook in simplified characters. A free companion website provides all the audio for the course with a broad range of interactive exercises and additional resources for students' self-study, along with a comprehensive instructor's guide with teaching tips, assessment and homework material, and a full answer key.

Key changes to this new edition:

- This revised edition of level 2 introduces over 200 characters and over 400 new vocabulary items.

- Additional exercises in the workbooks and online support the expanded number of words and characters incorporated into the textbooks.

- New cross-references between the textbooks, workbooks, and companion website facilitate using all the resources in an integrated manner.

- The website has been redesigned and greatly enhanced.

Retaining its focus on communicative skills and the long-term retention of characters, the text is presented in simplified characters and pinyin with a gradual and phased removal of pinyin as specific characters are introduced and learned. This approach allows students to focus on the pronunciation and meaning of new words before the corresponding characters are introduced, ensuring they are guided and supported towards reading only in characters.

Claudia Ross is Professor Emerita of Chinese at the College of the Holy Cross, Massachusetts, USA. Her publications include *Modern Mandarin Chinese Grammar: A Practical Guide* (2014), co-authored with Jing-heng Sheng Ma; *Outline of Chinese Grammar* (2004); and *Traditional Chinese Tales: A Course in Intermediate Chinese* (2001).

Baozhang He is Associate Professor Emeritus of Chinese at the College of the Holy Cross, Massachusetts, USA. His publications include *Difficult Grammar Knots Unravelled* (2015), co-authored with Nansong Huang and Wenzi Hu and *Elementary Chinese* (2006), co-authored with Pei-Chia Chen.

Pei-Chia Chen is Lecturer and Academic Coordinator of the Chinese program at UC San Diego, USA. Her publications include *Elementary Chinese* (2006), co-authored with Baozhang He.

Meng Yeh is Teaching Professor in the Center for Languages and Intercultural Communication at Rice University, USA. Her publications include *Chaoyue: Advancing in Chinese* (2010) and *Communicating in Chinese: An Interactive Approach to Beginning Chinese, Student Lab Workbook* (1999).

D1245819

Modern Mandarin Chinese

The Routledge Course Workbook Level 2

Second edition

Claudia Ross, Baozhang He, Pei-Chia Chen, and Meng Yeh

Routledge
Taylor & Francis Group

LONDON AND NEW YORK

Second edition published 2022
by Routledge
4 Park Square, Milton Park, Abingdon, Oxon, OX14 4RN

and by Routledge
605 Third Avenue, New York, NY 10158

Routledge is an imprint of the Taylor & Francis Group, an informa business

© 2022 Claudia Ross, Baozhang He, Pei-Chia Chen, and Meng Yeh

The right of Claudia Ross, Baozhang He, Pei-Chia Chen, and Meng Yeh to be identified as authors of this work has been asserted by them in accordance with sections 77 and 78 of the Copyright, Designs and Patents Act 1988.

First edition published by Routledge 2012

British Library Cataloguing-in-Publication Data
A catalogue record for this book is available from the British Library

Library of Congress Cataloging-in-Publication Data
Names: Ross, Claudia, author. | He, Baozhang, 1955– author. | Chen, Pei-Chia, author. | Ye, Meng, 1950– author.
Title: Modern Mandarin Chinese : the Routledge course workbook level 2 / Claudia Ross, Baozhang He, Pei-Chia Chen, and Meng Yeh.
Other titles: Routledge course in modern Mandarin Chinese. Workbook level 2 : Simplified characters
Description: 2nd edition. | Abingdon, Oxon ; New York, NY : Routledge, 2021. | Includes bibliographical references and index.
Identifiers: LCCN 2020048668 (print) | LCCN 2020048669 (ebook) | ISBN 9781138101166 (paperback) | ISBN 9781315657165 (ebook)
Subjects: LCSH: Chinese language—Textbook for foreign speakers—English. | Mandarin dialects.
Classification: LCC PL1129.E5 R682 2021 (print) | LCC PL1129.E5 (ebook) | DDC 495.182/421—dc23
LC record available at https://lccn.loc.gov/2020048668
LC ebook record available at https://lccn.loc.gov/2020048669

ISBN: 978-1-138-10116-6 (pbk)
ISBN: 978-1-315-65716-5 (ebk)

Typeset in Scala
by Apex CoVantage, LLC

Access the companion website: www.routledge.com/cw/ross

Contents

How to use the resources in this course to learn Chinese   vii

Lesson 17 Xuǎn 课 *Selecting courses*   1

    Focus on literacy   1

    Focus on structure   6

    Focus on communication   10

Lesson 18 选 zhuānyè *Selecting a major*   16

    Focus on literacy   16

    Focus on structure   20

    Focus on communication   27

Lesson 19 Shōushi 房间 *Straightening up the room*   33

    Focus on literacy   33

    Focus on structure   37

    Focus on communication   42

Lesson 20 看 bìng *Getting sick and seeing a doctor*   47

    Focus on literacy   47

    Focus on structure   52

    Focus on communication   56

Lesson 21 天气和气候变化 *Weather and climate change*   62

    Focus on literacy   62

    Focus on structure   66

    Focus on communication   72

Lesson 22 Duànliàn 身体 *Working out*   78

    Focus on literacy   78

    Focus on structure   83

    Focus on communication   91

Lesson 23 Guàng jiē *Going shopping*   99

    Focus on literacy   99

    Focus on structure   103

    Focus on communication   106

Lesson 24 Jiǎn 价，打折 *Discounts and bargains*   113

    Focus on literacy   113

    Focus on structure   117

    Focus on communication   121

Lesson 25 过春节 *Celebrating the New Year festival*   127

    Focus on literacy   127

    Focus on structure   131

    Focus on communication   136

How to use the resources in this course to learn Chinese

This course consists of a textbook, workbook, and website with a wealth of material designed to help you to learn to speak Mandarin and read and write in Chinese. The following is an overview of the resources, with suggestions to help you do your best work.

Textbook. The textbook presents new material and explanations.

- Stroke order flow charts show you how to write each new character, stroke by stroke. The *Narrative* and *Dialogue* illustrate the use of words and structures, as well as the cultural conventions of communication associated with each topic.

- *Use and Structure* notes explain how new structures function and how structures and phrases are used.

- *Sentence Pyramids* show you how words and phrases are grouped into sentences and help you to understand Chinese word order.

- *Narrative Structure* explanations show you how to organize information into cohesive essays for different communicative functions.

- *Language FAQs* and *Notes on Chinese Culture* provide additional information about language use and Chinese culture related to the topic of the lesson.

Workbook. The workbook provides exercises that you can do as homework or in class to practice the words, structures, and themes introduced in each lesson. These include:

- *Focus on Literacy*
- *Focus on Structure*
- *Focus on Communication*

Website. Resources include:

- *Listening for Information* (*Listening Comprehension*) *exercises*
- *Structure Drills* to help you strengthen spoken production and oral comprehension of new structures and vocabulary.
- Audio recordings of vocabulary introduced in each lesson.
- Audio recordings of the *Sentence Pyramids*.
- Downloadable *Character Practice Sheets*
- *Focus on Radicals* files for each lesson, with the characters sorted by radical.

Study Tips:

- Learn vocabulary and characters for each section of the text before your classroom lesson and before you begin working on the workbook exercises. If you don't know the words in a lesson, you can't participate in class and you cannot do the homework. Vocabulary and characters are organized by narrative and dialogue part, making it easier for you to focus on the new words and characters for each section of text. *Regularly review* vocabulary and characters from earlier lessons. Use the resources provided with this course to help you study. Download the character practice sheets from the course website to practice writing characters. Pay attention to the stroke order presented on the practice sheets so that you learn to write characters correctly. Using the same stroke order each time you write a character helps you to remember the character. Conversely, if you write a character differently each time you write it, your brain will have a hard time remembering it. Listen to the vocabulary audio files on the website to help you review vocabulary. Quiz yourself by using the files as dictation, and aim to write each word you hear with accurate pinyin and tones.

- Learn the structures. *Focus on Structure* exercises in the workbook are cross-referenced to specific *Use and Structure* notes. Read each *Use and Structure* note before you do each exercise, and follow the model sentences in each note as you complete your work. Work through the *Sentence Pyramids* in the textbook to see how phrases are built up into sentences in Chinese. Use the *Sentence Pyramids* in the textbook and website to test yourself, translating the Chinese column into English and checking your answers, and then translating the English column into Chinese. Listen to the *Sentence Pyramids* on the website and use them as dictation practice, testing your ability to accurately write and interpret what you hear. Work through the *Structure Drills* on the website to practice new structures on your own.

- Use the *Listening for Information* exercises to develop your listening comprehension skills. Do not expect to understand listening files on your first try. Be prepared to listen to the same passage multiple times in order to train your brain to understand what it hears. Use the pause button as you listen to help you to focus on shorter segments of a longer passage. Help your brain to focus on information by reading the instructions and the answer choices before you listen. The *Structure Drills* provided on the website will also help you to develop your listening skills along with your control of new structures and vocabulary.

- The *Focus on Communication* exercises will guide you to read and write longer passages in Chinese. The *Focus on Literacy* section of the workbook also includes reading passages that challenge you to read around characters that you do not know, and to make inferences based on the text. While reading, identify the sentence structures in each passage so that you know how words and phrases in the text are related. Identify word boundaries so that you group characters correctly, and look for connecting words that tell you if the text is presenting a sequence, or a description, or an explanation, etc. Before you write, think of what you want to say, and jot down the Chinese structures that you can use to express your meaning. Think of how you want to organize your ideas, and make a list of the connecting words or structures you need for the organization you are planning. After you write, proofread your work to make sure that the characters you have written or typed are correct and are the ones that you intended. When reading or writing, if you cannot remember a character or a vocabulary item, use this as an opportunity to review.

If you spend the time you need to prepare and review, you will have a successful and satisfying Chinese learning experience. Good luck in your studies!

Lesson 17 Xuǎn 课 Selecting courses

🎧 Listening and speaking

Listening comprehension exercises, structure drills for listening and speaking practice, audio files for vocabulary, and the sentence pyramids are on the companion website.

Focus on literacy

Additional exercises focusing on Chinese characters are on the companion website.

1. First two strokes

Consult the stroke order flow chart in the textbook and write the first **two** strokes of each of the following characters.

a. 陪   f. 系

b. 校   g. 乐

c. 用   h. 因

d. 所   i. 帮

e. 兴   j. 钟

2. Radicals

Here are some of the characters introduced in this lesson.

a. Write each character in the row next to its radical.

挣	因	钟	作	活	关	帮	系
直	校	兴	陪	惯	担	共	题

扌	
木	
钅	
口	
忄	
讠	
亻	
八	
氵	
巾	
目	
纟	
页	
阝	

b. For some of these characters, the radical helps to identify the meaning of the character. Circle all of the characters for which this is the case. How is the meaning of the radical in each of these characters related to meaning of the character in which it occurs? Consult the *Focus on Radicals* file for Lesson 17 on the companion website as you do this exercise.

3.　Find the bùjiàn (部件 component parts)

The following are characters introduced in this and previous lessons along with a list of **bùjiàn** (部件 *component parts*) that recur in many characters. Some of these component parts serve as the radical in the character in which they occur, and some do not. Write each character next to a component part that it includes. You may use a character more than once.

但	钟	市	唱	惯	太	活	帮	兴
真	贵	昨	音	因	直	想	话	作

bùjiàn	characters
亻	
八	
目	
十	
日	
乍	
舌	
贝	
大	
中	
巾	

4. Reading for basic information

This passage contains some characters and words that we have not yet learned, but follow the instructions and you will be able to read it for basic information.

今年夏天放暑假的时候，我从中国回美国看我的父母。我有半年多没有看见他们了，很想他们。他们当然也很想我。到了家，我妈妈问我最想吃什么，她可以去买给我。我说我很想吃的东西，不用去买，家里一定有很多。我跟他们说我刚到中国的时候，最不习惯的就是吃北京的早饭。我觉得北京的早饭油很多，不太健康。我喜欢美国的谷物早餐，加一些牛奶就可以了。又方便，又健康。中国虽然有谷物早餐，可是很贵。爸爸说："对。谷物早餐在宿舍吃就可以了。又可以起得很晚，又可以不去餐厅。"我说："爸爸，你上大学的时候就这样吧。"

a. Where did the author travel from and where did s/he go? What key words do you need to answer this question? Underline the sentence that provides this information, and write the information in English here:

_____

b. This text includes two different two-character words for "breakfast." We have learned one of them. Find and circle the word for breakfast that we have learned. Then circle another, similar word that you think may mean breakfast. How are the words alike and why do you think the second one means breakfast? What clues are there in the text that indicate that this word means breakfast?

c. The author gives his opinion about Beijing breakfast. Put a box around the sentence where he expresses his opinion, and another box around the word that tells you he is expressing his opinion.

d. Where does this conversation take place? How do you know? (Hint: You are going to have to make an inference based on information in the text.)

e. When does this conversation take place? How do you know?

f. The author says: 我说我很想吃的东西，不用去买.

我很想吃的东西 consists of a noun preceded by a description of the noun. What is the noun that is being described? What does the description say about that noun? Why does the author say "不用去买"?

g. In the passage, the author's father explains what he thinks about 谷物早餐. Double underline the part of the passage where he gives his opinion, and provide two words in English or Mandarin to summarize his opinion.

5. Using dictionary skills to find key words

To understand the finer details of the passage above, we have to look up a few words. Follow the instructions for looking up characters in a Chinese dictionary in Lesson 17 of the textbook, and look up the following characters:

a. 油

pronunciation:

meaning:

b. 健

pronunciation:

meaning:

the two-character phrase in which it occurs in this passage:

c. 谷物 (look up 谷 and find the word 谷物 in the list of words that begin with 谷 in this entry.

pronunciation:

meaning:

The four character phrase in which it occurs in this passage:

6. Proofread 大为's email

大为 has written this email to a friend back home but he has typed 13 different characters wrong (some more than once). Read the passage aloud, circle the mistakes, and correct them on the answer sheet below. If the same mistake occurs more than once, count it as a single mistake.

学期钱天就开学了。我非常忙。 这个学期我 xuǎn 了四们课，一们音东科，一们法问课， 还有两们中文课。音乐课早上八店中就开始，所以我得早一点七 chuáng。我七 chuáng 的时后我的 tóngwū 还再 shuì 觉。我美天上课一前现吃一点东西。

a.	b.	c.	d.	e.	f.	g.
h.	i.	j.	k.	l.	m.	

7. Scrambled sentences

Rewrite these phrases as sentences, putting the words in the correct order to match the English translations.

a. 都/ 的时候/忙 / 学生/非常/ 刚/学期/开始

When the semester just begins, the students are all extremely busy.

b. 音乐/一直/她 / 有兴 qu/对 / 很

She has always been very interested in music.

c. 习惯/都 / 学校/我 / 在/的 / 吃饭/cāntīng/每天/不

I am not used to eating at the school cafeteria every day.

8. Where is tomorrow?

Read the following passage and translate it into English.

明天的明天是后天。"后天" 的 "后" 是 "后 biān" 的 "后"。中文的后天不是在你的后 biān。中文的后天是在你的前 biān。后天还没有到呢。昨天的昨天是前天。"前天" 的 "前" 是 "前 biān" 的 "前"。中文的前天不是在你的前 biān。中文的前天在你的后 biān。前天已经过去了。

9. Typing practice

Type the following sentences in Chinese characters and translate them into English.

a. Wǒ gāng huí xuéxiào.

b. Yīnwèi wǒ hěn xǐhuān tīng yīnyuè, suǒyǐ zhè gè xuéqī wǒ xiǎng xuǎn (选) yī mén yīnyuè kè.

c. Wǒ tīngshuō Zhōngwén kè yǒu yīdiǎn nán, kěshì wǒ yīzhí juéde Zhōngwén hěn yǒu yòng.

Focus on structure

1.   Everyone is busy (Use and structure 17.2)

It is Sunday evening. Everyone in the house is so busy concentrating on what they are doing that no one hears the doorbell ringing. Describe what everyone is busying doing using 忙 **zhe.**

(cooking) a. 妈妈	(surfing the internet) b. 爸爸
(doing homework) c. 小明	(talking on the phone) d. 小明的姐姐

a. _____

b. _____

c. _____

d. _____

2.   回来，回国 (Use and structure 17.3)

Here are the names of some Chinese students studying at our school. Write a sentence in Mandarin for each one, stating when they went back to their home country (回国) and when they came back (回来).

	went home	came back
a. Zhái Yàn	June 9	August 14
b. 王 Jú	May 29	September 1
c. Chén 文	July 2	August 31

a. _____

b. _____

c. _____

3.   I haven't done that for a long time (Use and structure 17.4)

Yáng 明明 has been busy working on a school project for two months now. He finally turned it in today and is complaining about all of the things he hasn't done. Write each of his complaints in Mandarin, using the example as your guide.

Example: watching movies, two months → 我有两个月没有看电 yǐng 了。

a. sing karaoke, one and a half months→

b. Call my girlfriend, 10 days→

c. Go home, one month→

d. Watch television, three weeks→

e. Take a shower, two days→

f. Sleep, 25 hours→

4.   Indirect questions and reported questions (Use and structure 17.8)

张大为 asked 谢国强 a lot of questions on the way to the bookstore. Afterwards, 国强 told his friend **Màikè** what 张大为 had asked. Here are the English versions of the questions. Rewrite them *in Chinese*, as in the example.

Example: He asked me if the bookstore was open. 张大为问我书店开不开门。

a. He asked me what time the movie begins.

b. He asked me if the math teacher was strict.

c. He asked me whether that Chinese book is useful.

d. He asked me if that Japanese class was hard.

e. He asked me how many courses I am taking this semester.

5.   More indirect questions (Use and structure 17.8)

Rewrite <u>the question part</u> of each dialogue exchange as a sentence with an indirect question, as in the example.

Example:

国强：你这个学期上中文课吗？

大为：上。

→ 国强问大为他这个学期<u>上不上</u>中文课。

a. 小文: 你会开车吗？

美丽：不会。

→_____

b. 谢太太：你们吃过 jiǎo 子吗？

王 Màikè：吃过。我很喜欢。

→_____

c. 美丽：你昨天看的那个电 yǐng 有意思吗？

小文：非常有意思。

→_____

d. 王老师：你觉得中国文 huà 课难不难？

大为：不太难，只是考试很多。

→_____

6.   What did they say? (Use and structure 17.6)

Rewrite <u>the reply</u> in each of the dialogue exchanges in Exercise 5 as a sentence stating what the person said, as in the example. Use the word supplied in parentheses in your sentence.

Example:

国强：你这个学期上中文课吗？

大为：上。

→（说）大为<u>跟国强说</u>他这个学期上中文课。

a. (告诉)：_____

b. (说)：_____

c. (告诉)：_____

d. (说)：_____

7.   一点 or 有一点 (Use and structure 17.13)

Complete each sentence in Mandarin to match the English translation, using 一点 or 有一点 as appropriate.

a. 这本书太贵了。*Can it be a little bit cheaper?*

b. *I've heard that this class is a little hard.* 老师也很 yán。

c. *It's already a little late.* 我 yīnggāi 回 sùshè 了。

d. 明天是星期天。 *You can wake up a little later.*

e. 这个 jiǎo 子很好吃。   *You should eat a little more.*

f. *My home is a little far from the subway station.* 我到车站去接你吧。

g. 你说话说得太快了。   *Please speak a little slower.*

8.   Interested or not interested? (Use and structure 17.14)

The following is a list of things that **Gāo Měilì** is interested in and a list of things that she is not interested in. Ask her if she is interested in each of these things, and write her response to each of your questions.

Gāo Měilì is interested in . . .	Gāo Měilì is **not** interested in
a. French culture	b. politics
c. Korean music	d. dancing
e. math	f. German literature （文学）
g. environmental studies	h. physics

a. Question:

   Answer:

b. Question:

   Answer:

c. Question:

   Answer:

d. Question:

   Answer:

e. Question:

   Answer:

f. Question:

   Answer:

g. Question:

   Answer:

h. Question:

   Answer:

9.   Translation challenge I (Use and structure 17.2, 17.9, 17.12, 17.14)

Translate these passages into English.

a. 妈妈：Shù 学很有用。 这个学期你 yīnggāi xuǎn 一门 shù 学课。

   Hái 子：好。我对 shù 学很有兴 qu，不过我听说我们学校的 shù 学老师都 bǐjiào yán。

b. 小王：我前天给你打电话你不在。你忙 zhe 做什么呢？

   小马：Xīn 学期快要开始了。我忙 zhe 买课本呢。

c. 老师：你自己的功课得自己做。不要请别的学生帮你做。

10.   Translation challenge II (Use and structure 17.9, 17.10, 17.14)

Translate these sentences into Mandarin. Use characters wherever we have learned them.

a. This semester I'm taking five courses: one music class, one American culture class, two Japanese language courses, and one Japanese culture class. I have three classes every day.

b. 国强: Do you have Chinese homework every day?

   大为: Yes. This Chinese teacher is very strict. We have homework every day. However, we only have two exams each semester.

c. Guóqiáng asked me if Měilì has a boyfriend. I told him that I'm not interested in other people's lives.

Focus on communication

Additional Focus on communication exercises as well as classroom activities for spoken communication are on the Teachers' Resource website.

1.   What do you say?

What do you say in each of the following situations? Type your answers, using characters where we have learned them.

a. You want to find out if the coffee shop is open right now.

b. You want to express your long-term interest in Chinese music.

c. You want to tell your roommate that you heard that the food at the school cafeteria is rather expensive.

d. You want to find out how many courses your roommate is taking this semester.

e. You want to explain why your Chinese is a bit rusty. (The reason is that you haven't spoken Chinese for two months.)

f. You turn down a movie invitation because you have to use that time to prepare for a physics exam.

g. You advise your friend to go to other places to eat since this place is not appropriate.

2. Mini-dialogues (Use and structure 17.5, 17.10, 17.11)

Complete each dialogue, using the structure in parentheses.

a. A: 这个工作钱不多，离你家也很远，你为什么喜欢？

   B: _____ (因为)

b. A: 你觉得你的学校怎么样？

   B: _____ (. . . 只是 . . .)

c. A: **Zāogāo**, 我忘了做功课，老师一 **dìng** 会不高兴。

   B: _____ (没关系)

d. A: 听说李老师很 **yán**, 是不是？你上过他的课，你觉得呢？

   B: _____ (不过)

e. A: 我以为你说你打 **suàn** 去法国 **lǚyóu**？你怎么没去？

   B: _____, 可是_____, 所以

   zuì 后我没去。 **(yuán 来)**

3. Multiple choice (Use and structure 17.5, 17.11)

Select the best expression to complete each sentence and translate your sentences into English.

a. 我喜欢吃家常 **cài**，____ 我做得不好。

   1. 所以

   2. 因为

   3. 可是

English: _____

b. ____ 星期五早上我要打工，_____我不 **néng xuǎn** 这门课。

   1. 因为 . . . 所以

   2. Suī 然 . . . 可是

   3. 因为 . . . 不过

English: _____

c. 书店现在没开门，所以_____

   1. 今天是星期天。

   2. 一会儿就开了。

   3. 我不 **néng** 去买课本。

English: _____

d. **Suī** 然我已经学了三年的中文了。可是_____

   1. 我一直对中文很有兴 **qù**。

   2. 我还没去过中国。

   3. 我每天都有中文课。

English: _____

e. 因为快考试了，所以____

   1. 很多人在图书馆学习。

   2. 我下个星期三有考试。

   3. 听说老师 **bǐjiào yán**。

English: _____

4.   A conversation between Zhang Dawei and Wang Maike

Part I. Fill in the blanks with the correct word chosen from the following.

只是	自己	一 **dìng**	门	刚
在	没关系	**zhe**	有	早就

王**Màikè:** 大为，我＿＿＿＿几个星期没有看见你了。你＿＿＿＿忙什么？

张大为: 我忙＿＿＿＿学习呢。这个学期我 **xuǎn** 了几＿＿＿＿**bǐjiào** 难的课。每天都有很多功课。我常常没有时间想别的事。**Zāogāo!** 我忘了买中文课本。 学校书店的书都太贵，我真不想＿＿＿＿那儿买。

Màikè: 我听说学友书店的书都很 **piányi**，＿＿＿＿有一 点远。你＿＿＿＿ 兴**qu**吗？我 ＿＿＿＿想去看看了，不过我不想＿＿＿＿一个人去。

大为: 真的吗？有点远＿＿＿＿，我＿＿＿＿买车，我们可以开我的新车去。

Part II. Q&A. Read the previous dialogue. Then, answer the questions in Mandarin.

a. 大为为什么忙 **zhe** 学习？＿＿＿＿＿＿＿＿＿＿＿＿＿＿＿＿＿＿＿＿

b. 大为这个学期上不上中文课？你怎么知道？＿＿＿＿＿＿＿＿＿＿＿＿＿＿

c. **Màikè** 为什么觉得学友书店 **bǐjiào héshì?**＿＿＿＿＿＿＿＿＿＿＿＿＿＿＿

d. **Zuì** 后他们打 **suàn** 去哪个书店买书？＿＿＿＿＿＿＿＿＿＿＿＿＿＿＿

5.   Sequence of events (Use and structure 17.7, 17.11)

Indicate the sequence of events in Dawei's morning in complete sentences based on the illustrations and the prompt for each sentence.

a. This is 大为's morning routine: (use "先...再...然后... **zuì**后...")

sequence: 1. 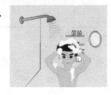   3.

2.    4.

a. 每天早上起 **chuáng** 以后大为＿＿＿＿＿＿＿＿＿＿＿＿＿＿＿＿＿＿＿＿

b. This is what 小明 does after dinner. (Use 先, 然后， Verb 以前...)
sequence:

1.

3.

2.

4.

b. 吃了晚饭以后，小明_____

c. This is what 美美 plans to do this summer. (Use 一...就..., 然后，以后就...)
sequence:

summer school   →   travel   →   return home

c. 一**fàng shǔjià** 美美就_____

d. A perfect day at __ (your choice of place) ___:
Imagine you have an out-of-town guest. Plan a perfect day to show him/her around. Where would you take them; what would you do? What's the first and the last thing you would do? Use the words that describe sequence (see above) to connect the activities.

_____

_____

_____

_____

_____

6. Writing I

You are writing to your favorite high school teacher to let him/her know how you've been since you entered college. In this paragraph, talk about the classes you are taking and the impact they have on your life this semester. The following is a list of expressions that you can use in your paragraph. Include at least FOUR of them.

因为 ... 所以	有(一) 点	只是	有帮 zhù	zhòng 要
忙 zhe	不过	**bǐjiào**	有用	**xuǎn**

_____

_____

_____

_____

_____

_____

7. Writing II

You want to convince your best friend to take this particular course (your choice) with you. Explain what's good about this class and the benefit of taking it with a friend.

The following is a list of expressions that you can use in your paragraph. Include at least THREE of them.

因为 ... 所以	**bǐjiào**	一 **dìng**	对 ... 有 兴 qù
再说	有帮 zhù	有用	**xuǎn**

_____

_____

_____

_____

_____

_____

Lesson 18 选 zhuānyè
Selecting a major

🎧 Listening and speaking

Listening comprehension exercises, structure drills for listening and speaking practice, audio files for vocabulary, and the sentence pyramids are on the companion website.

Focus on literacy

Additional exercises focusing on Chinese characters are on the companion website.

1. First two strokes

Consult the stroke order flow chart in the textbook and write the first **two** strokes of each of the following characters.

a.	适	f.	爱	
b.	定	g.	数	
c.	利	h.	选	
d.	级	i.	累	
e.	最	j.	出	

2. Radicals

The following are characters that we have learned in this and previous lessons.

a. Write each character in the row next to its radical.

同	换	定	经	最	济	别	家	起	挣	到
趣	能	利	活	合	选	系	级	洗	刚	累

糸/纟	
宀	
辶	
口	
日	
刂	
走	
氵	
扌	
月	

b. For some of these characters, the radical helps to identify the meaning of the character. Circle all of the characters for which this is the case. How is the meaning of the radical in each of these characters related to meaning of the character in which it occurs? Consult the *Focus on Radicals* file for Lesson 18 on the companion website as you do this exercise.

3. Find the bùjiàn (部件 component parts)

The following are characters introduced in this and previous lessons along with a list of **bùjiàn** (部件 *component parts*) that recur in many characters. Some of these component parts serve as the radical in the character in which they occur, and some do not. Write each character next to a component part that it includes. You may use a character more than once.

趣　帮　同　累　果　题　都　昨　爱　数　最

男　明　作　烦　合　校　怎　陪　经　但　定

bùjiàn	characters
木	
日	
又	
乍	
阝	
糸/纟	
耳	
田	
页	
口	

4.   Reading for basic information

This passage contains some characters and words that we have not yet learned, but follow the instructions and you will be able to read it for basic information.

你对哪门课有兴趣，不一定要选那个专业。选专业跟很多方面有关系。第一，那个专业难不难。如果很难，你一定学不好。第二，那个专业有用没有。没有用的东西为什么要学呢？最后，那个专业容易不容易找工作。学了一个专业，可是没有工作有什么用呢？这就是为什么专业跟兴趣有关系，可是关系不大。

a. Circle the word 专业 every time it occurs in the text.

b. For each occurrence, indicate whether it is the subject of the sentence (S) or object of a verb (O).

c. When it is the object of a verb, put a box around the verb.

d. When it is the subject of a sentence, what does the sentence say or ask about 专业?

e. What does the author conclude about 专业? Underline the phrase that identifies the author's words as a conclusion.

f. What do you think 专业 means? Why?

5.   Using dictionary skills to find key words

Check your answer to 4(f) by looking up the word 专业 in a Chinese character dictionary. Follow the instructions for looking up characters in a Chinese dictionary in Lesson 17 of the textbook and look up 专。

a. Write its pinyin pronunciation here:

b. Find the word 专业 in the list of words following the character 专 and write its pinyin pronunciation and meaning here:

6.   Proofread 大为's email

大为 has written this email to his older brother, but he has typed 11 characters wrong, two of them more than once. Read the passage aloud, circle the mistakes, and correct them on the answer sheet below.

因为我一真对书学很有兴去，所以这个学七我先了两们数学可。可是 **dì** 一个考是以后，我的考是分数不太好。下可以后我去找老师。老师跟我话，**dì** 一个考试的分数好不好没有关西。如果你一直很用功，一定能字好，一定能考好。

1.	2.	3.	4.	5.	6.
7.	8.	9.	10.	11.	12.

7.   Scrambled sentences

Rewrite these phrases as sentences, putting the words in the correct order to match the English translations.

a. 选/bǐjiào/我/ 我/每个/强 / 都/数学课/所以/因为/数学/学期 /一门

   Since I am relatively strong in math, I take a math class every semester.

b. 兴趣/你 / 什么/有 / 最/对

   What are you most interested in?

c. 忙/一年级/每天/大学生/ 非常/都 / 的

   First-year college students are extremely busy every day.

d. 以前/行 / 功课/行 / fù习/我们/图书馆/不 / 考试/去

   Let's go to the library to review the course work before the test, okay?

e. 工作/没 / 那样/有 / 的/兴趣/对 / 我

   I am not interested in that kind of job.

8.   Typing practice

Type the following sentences in Chinese characters and translate them into English.

a. Guóqiáng shì xuéxiào yīniánjí de xuésheng.

b. Tā měitiān yào qù shàng kè, yě yào dǎ gōng, suǒyǐ tā hěn máng, yǒu de kǎoshì fēnshù yě bù hǎo.

c. Tā yě xiǎng zhǐ shàng kè, bù gōngzuò.

d. Zhèyàng tā de kǎoshì fēnshù huì hǎo yīdiǎn.

e. Kěshì tā yīdìng děi qù gōngzuò.

f. Qù gōngzuò, zhèng yī diǎn qián, tā cái kěyǐ shàng xué.

Focus on structure

1.   There is a connection between these things (Use and structure 18.1)

Write a sentence for each of the following pairs of situations, saying that there is a relationship between them, as in the example.

Example:

A	B
选 **zhuānyè**	你的爱好

选 **zhuānyè** 跟你的爱好有关系。

A	B
a. 考试的分数	考试难不难
b. 学生用功不用功	**chéngjì** 好 **huài**
c. 喜欢不喜欢这门课	老师
d. 老师 **yán** 不 **yán**	学生用功不用功
e. 选什么课	你的兴趣

2.   Is there a connection? (Use and structure 18.1)

Rewrite the sentences you wrote in Exercise 1 as questions, and translate your questions into English.

a. _____

_____

b. _____

_____

c. _____

_____

d. _____

_____

e. _____

_____

3.   There isn't any connection (Use and structure 18.1)

Answer "no" to each of the questions that you wrote in Exercise 2 in complete Mandarin sentences.

a. _____

b. _____

c. _____

d. _____

e. _____

4. Describing nouns, Part I (Use and structure 18.2)

Using the pattern **description** 的 **noun**, translate each of the following noun phrases into Mandarin. The main noun is underlined in each phrase.

Example:

the <u>classes</u> that I selected: 我选的课

a. the <u>cell phone</u> that I bought yesterday

b. the <u>Chinese restaurant</u> that we went to

c. the <u>movie</u> that I watched

d. the <u>students</u> who select a major in economics

e. the <u>car</u> that she drives

5. Describing nouns, Part II (Use and structure 18.2)

Translate the following noun phrases into English.

a. 我买的书

b. 我昨天看的那本书

c. jiāo 我中文的老师

d. 他昨天喝 的 jiǔ

e. 我昨天看的电 yǐng

f. 她上个星期买的中文书

g. 我的同 wū 昨天买的书

h. cānjiā quán 国考试的高中生

6. Describing nouns, Part III (Use and structure 18.2)

The noun phrases that you translated in Exercise 5 above occur as the subject or object of the verb in these sentences. Translate these sentences into English, referring to your translations in Exercise 5.

a. 我买的书都 bǐjiào 贵。

_____

b. 我昨天看的那本书很好。

_____

c. 他是 jiāo 我中文的老师。

_____

d. 他昨天喝 的 jiǔ 是法国 jiǔ。

_____

e. 我昨天看的电 yǐng 没有意思。

_____

f. 他上个星期买的中文书非常 piányi。

_____

g. 我的同 wū 昨天买的书是一年级的中文书。

_____

h. Cānjiā quán 国考试的高中生都很 jǐn张。

_____

7. Describing nouns, Part IV (Use and structure 18.2)

These sentences each contain a noun phrase with a verb description. Translate them
into English. The noun phrase and description are underlined.

a. <u>The fruit that you gave me (as a present)</u> is extremely delicious.

_____

b. <u>Students who graduate from college</u> often go to big cities to find jobs.

_____

c. Students <u>who returned to their home country this summer</u> are coming back
tomorrow.

_____

8. Describing nouns, Part V (Use and structure 18.2)

Put square brackets around the description clauses in each of the following sentences,
circle the main verb, and then translate the sentences into English.

a. Cānjiā 考试的学生不一定都shēn请大学。

_____

b. 你认识的高中生喝不喝 píjiǔ?

_____

c. 帮她找工作的那个人已经在中国住了一年了。

_____

d. 你能不能给我 jièshào 昨天晚上跟你吃饭的那个人？

_____

9. Describing nouns, Part VI (Use and structure 18.2, 18.13)

The following noun phrases each contain a noun that is described by more than one description. Underline each description phrase, and then translate these noun phrases into English.

a. 我昨天买的很贵的手机

_____

b. 我昨天晚上看的很有意思的日本电 yǐng

_____

c. 这个学期选中文的美国学生

_____

d. 那两个 shēn 请去中国学习的大学生

_____

e. 我觉得最有意思的那些课

_____

f. 我们刚认识的学数学的那个人

_____

10. 一bān (一般): Exchanging information about Chinese and American people (Use and structure 18.6)

大为 and 国强 are exchanging information about Chinese and American people. Translate 国强's information into English, and 大为's information into Mandarin, using 一**bān** in each Chinese sentence.

a. 国强: 中国人一**bān** 只有一个孩子.

_____

b. 国强: 中国人一**bān** 喜欢上网买东西。

_____

c. 国强：中国大学生一**bān** 都学过一点英文。

_____

d. Dawei: Americans generally have two or three children.

_____

e. Dawei: American college students generally select majors when they are sophomores. (subject + time when + action)

_____

f. 大为: Americans in general can't use chopsticks to eat Chinese food.

_____

11. Rhetorical questions with 难道 . . . 吗？ *Do you mean to say . . . ?* (Use and structure 18.5)

大为 and 国强 are a little surprised about some of the things they learned about each other's countries. Translate 国强's responses into English, and 大为's responses into Mandarin, using 难道 . . . 吗？ in each of the Chinese sentences.

a. 国强：难道美国人不会用 kuài 子吗？

_____

b. 国强；难道上大学的时候你的 zhuānyè 还没 jué 定吗？

_____

c. 大为：Do you mean to say that Chinese college students can all speak English?

_____

d. 大为：Do you mean to say that Chinese people don't have siblings (xiōng弟姐妹)?

_____

12. Ràng (让): What are you allowed to do? (Use and structure 18.7)

大为 is writing his parents about his life in China. Help him by completing each sentence, using **ràng** (让) or **bù ràng** (不让) in each sentence.

a. 老师 do not let the students look at their cell phones in class (when attending class).

_____

b. 我的朋友 doesn't let me use his cell phone.

_____

c. 我的同 wū lets me listen to music before going to sleep.

_____

d. 学校 does not let students drink beer in the dorms.

_____

13. From this perspective (Use and structure 18.9)

Translate the following sentences into English.

1. 我的同 wū 在学习方面很 cōng 明，可是在生活方面很 bèn。我在 sùshè 要帮他做很多事 qing。

_____

2. 在选 zhuānyè 这方面，你最好问问你的爸爸妈妈和别的同学，不要自己 jué 定。

_____

3. 在中文和中国文 huà 这些方面国强帮大为，在英文和音乐方面国强常常请大为帮他。

_____

4. Suī 然国强常常帮大为学中文，可是在中文 yǔfǎ 方面国强也不懂。他只知道怎么说。

_____

14. Translation challenge I

Translate the following sentences into English. Begin by identifying the structures used in the sentence, including noun descriptions. The first sentence is outlined for you.

a. 美国的高中生在 bìyè 以前 cānjiā 不 cānjiā quán 国的考试? (___以前, ____的考试)

_____

b. 很多美国的大学生觉得喝 jiǔ 跟学习 chéngjì 没有关系。最重要的是喝 jiǔ 以后不要开车，学习的时候要用功。

_____

c. 我的爱好和兴趣是音乐和唱歌，可是选音乐 zhuānyè jiāng 来不容易找工作。我 yīnggāi 怎么 bàn 呢?

_____

d. 上大学为什么要选 zhuānyè 呢? 很多大学生 bìyè 以后的工作跟他的 zhuānyè 没有关系。

_____

e. Zhuānyè 没有好 huài，可是有的容易，有的难。为什么有很多学生要选很难的 zhuānyè 呢?

_____

f. 我快要 bìyè 了，开始 shēn 请工作。如果大学 bìyè 以后没有合适的工作，怎么 bàn 呢？

_____

g. 我昨天在图书馆认识的那个中国学生跟我说，如果我在学习中文方面有问题，我可以打电话问他。

_____

15. Translation challenge II

Translate these sentences into Mandarin, using the phrase or structure provided.

a. This matter is none of your business. (关系)

_____

b. She is the best teacher in our school. (最)

_____

c. Before you select your major, you should think about what you want to do in the future. (以前)

_____

d. The strongest students do not necessarily make the most money. (不一定)

_____

e. If you select a major that you don't like, you will feel tired. (如果)

_____

f. I've heard that you are interested in Chinese economics. Do you think that in the future you will study in China? (兴趣)

_____

g. Yes. I plan to go to China to study before I graduate college. After I graduate I will go back again and look for work. (以前，以后)

_____

h. In what ways are applying to an American college and applying to a Chinese college different?

_____

i. What do you do if your score on the national college exam is not good?

_____

You can wait until next year and take it again.

Focus on communication

> Additional Focus on communication exercises as well as classroom activities for spoken communication are on the Teachers' Resource website.

1.   What do you say?

What do you say in each of the following situations? Type your answers, using characters where we have learned them.

a. You want to tell your friend who just did really badly on a test that grades are not the most important thing.

b. You wonder what you should do because economics is not a major that you are interested in.

c. You want your friend to know that you had nothing to do with the situation (matter) that he mentioned.

d. You want to explain to your parents that math is not your strongest suit so you will not pick math as your major.

e. As a father, assure your son that if he begins to earn money right now, he can definitely afford his favorite car in the future.

f. You want to find out why your friend from China already knows her major before she enters college.

g. You encourage your brother to attend this career fair by saying that he can use this opportunity to find suitable jobs.

h. You were wondering if you could switch to a different teacher if you don't like the one you chose.

i. Tell your friend that you wanted to go, but your parents would not let you go to this concert.

2.   Mini-dialogues (Use and structure 18.1, 18.2, 18.8, 18.11)

Use the structure in parentheses to complete each mini-dialogue. You can respond in any way that makes sense and uses the targeted structure.

a. A: 这个 **jiǎo** 子真好吃！

   B: _____当然好吃！(description 的 Noun)

b. A: 你什么时候可以 **sòng** 我回家？

　　B: _____ (以后)

c. A: 你那么 **bèn**，当然没有女朋友！

　　B: _____ (A 跟 B 没有关系)

d. A: 中文、日文和法文哪个难？

　　B: _____ (最)

e. A: 如果书店没有我要的课本，怎么 **bàn?**

　　B: 别 **jǐn** 张，_____ (不会)

3.　Why and how? (Use and structure 18.12)

Fill in the blanks with 为什么, 这么, 怎么, or 怎么 **bàn** to complete each question. (Use 怎么 only once.) Then answer the question truthfully.

a. 从学校到你家_____走最快？

　　Answer: _____

b. 如果你很累，没有时间做饭，_____?

　　Answer: _____

c. 你 _____对中文有兴趣？

　　Answer: _____

d. 你想去法国 **lǚyóu**，可是你没有钱，_____?

　　Answer: _____

e. 上个学期你的 **chéngjì** 为什么_____ **zāogāo** (or _____ 好)?

　　Answer: _____

4.　Multiple choice

Select the expression that best completes each sentence and then translate the sentence into English.

a. 你去北京 **lǚyóu** 的时候，难道_____

　　1. 没有去 **Chángchéng (the Great Wall of China)** 吗？

　　2. 也去了别的地方。

　　3. 你喜欢北京吗？

English: _____

b. _____ 星期五早上我没有事，我_____ 跟你去那个新的书店。

　　1. 因为 . . . 所以

2. Suī 然 . . . 可是

3. 如果 . . . 就

English: _____

c. 我对数学没有兴趣，所以_____

1. 我的 **zhuānyè** 是数学。

2. 数学方面的课我都不选。

3. 我不能 **bìyè**。

English: _____

d. **Suī** 然有的 **zhuānyè jiāng** 来可以挣 **bǐjiào** 多的钱，但是_____

1. 我一直对经济很有兴趣 。

2. zhuānyè 和你的 **jiāng** 来有很大的关系。

3. 我觉得选一个你最喜欢的 **zhuānyè bǐjiào** 重要。

English: _____

e. 我们去学生 **cāntīng** 吃吧，学生 **cāntīng bǐjiào** 近，_____，他们的牛 **ròu** 面很好吃。

1. 再说

2. 不过

3. 只是

English: _____

5. 小王的 chéngjì

The following is Xiao Wang's report card from last semester. He tends to do well in the subjects that he has the most interest in and vice versa. Translate and answer the questions in Mandarin.

Chinese	Chinese culture	Economics	Mathematics	Chinese music
A+	A	B+	C–	A–

a. How many courses did Xiao Wang choose last semester?

Question: _____

Answer: _____

b. In which subject did Xiao Wang get the highest grade?

Question: _____

Answer: _____

c. What area was Xiao Wang strongest in?

Question: _____

Answer: _____

d. What factor influences (has something to do with) his grades?

Question: _____

Answer: _____

e. What course was Xiao Wang least interested in?

Question: _____

Answer: _____

f. In the future, what area can Xiao Wang look for a job in?

Question: _____

Answer: _____

6. Let's talk about our dreams (Use and structure 18.2)

You and a group of friends are talking about your dreams after graduation. Use the pattern **description** 的 **noun** to describe your dream job, ideal place to live, future partner and friends, etc.

Example sentence:

国强： *I want to find a job where (I) <u>can earn a lot of money</u>.*

我想找一个<u>可以挣很多钱</u>的工作。

Now it's your turn to talk about your dream –

a. 我想找一个_____ 的工作。

b. 我想住在一个_____ 的地方。

c. 我想找一个_____ 的男/女朋友。

d. 我想多认识一些 _____ 的朋友。

Here's what your friends said. Translate their replies into Mandarin:

a. 美丽： I want to live in a place that is <u>close to my parents</u>.

_____

b. 学友： I want to find a boyfriend who is <u>nice to me</u>.

_____

c. 爱明： I want to meet more friends who <u>like to watch movies</u>.

_____

7.   Do you agree? Why or why not?

Read each statement and write a simple response stating why you agree or do not agree with it. Start your sentence with: 我也觉得 / 我不觉得 + statement, 因为 . . . To support your statement with multiple reasons or scenarios, use 再说、还有, 如果 . . . 就 . . . , etc.

a. 选 **zhuānyè** 是大学生最重要的事 **qing**.

_____

_____

b. 选 **zhuānyè** 跟 **jiāng** 来的工作有很大的关系。

_____

_____

c. 如果大家都选这个 **zhuānyè**， 这个 **zhuānyè** 一定是最合适的。

_____

_____

d. 大学一年级和二年级选的课，可以帮你 **jué** 定你的 **zhuānyè**。

_____

_____

e. 如果选 **bǐjiào** 容易的 **zhuānyè**, 大学的生活会 **bǐjiào** 快乐.

_____

_____

8.   Writing I

Your high school teacher invited you back to share your experience with his current students. Write your script about how you decided on your major and why you chose it. You can use some of the answers you have used in the previous exercise. If you haven't decided on your major, explain what you are interested in and what major you might choose. Below is a list of expressions that you can use in your paragraph. Include at least FIVE of them.

因为 . . . 所以	**A** 跟 **B** 有关系	利用	**jué** 定	對 . . . 有兴趣
再說	如果 . . . 就	**bǐjiào**	有用	不过

_____

_____

_____

_____

_____

_____

_____

9. Writing II

Your high school teacher also wanted you to encourage the seniors to visit college campuses (看学校) before making a decision. Talk about the benefit and/or what to pay attention to when visiting a campus. Write from your own experience.

你可以利用这个机会_____

_____

_____

_____

然后再 **jué** 定你要不要 **shēn** 请这个学校。

Lesson 19 Shōushi 房间
Straightening up the room

🎧 Listening and speaking

Listening comprehension exercises, structure drills for listening and speaking practice, audio files for vocabulary, and the sentence pyramids are on the companion website.

Focus on literacy

Additional exercises focusing on Chinese characters are on the companion website.

1. First two strokes

Consult the stroke order flow chart in the textbook and write the first **two** strokes of each of the following characters.

a. 虽   f. 屋

b. 球   g. 虽

c. 脑   h. 末

d. 床   i. 等

e. 边   j. 宿

2. Radicals

a. The following are characters that we have learned through this lesson. Rewrite each character in the row next to its radical.

边	定	能	宿	周	房	妈	室	选	兴
脑	屋	放	舍	进	如	虽	数	客	奶

虫	
宀	
辶	
口	
月	
八	
户	
女	
尸	
攵	

b. For some of these characters, the radical helps to identify the meaning of the character. Circle all of the characters for which this is the case. How is the meaning of the radical in each of these characters related to meaning of the character in which it occurs? Consult the *Focus on Radicals* file for Lesson 19 on the companion website as you do this exercise.

3. Find the bùjiàn (部件 component parts)

The following are characters introduced in this and previous lessons along with a list of **bùjiàn** (部件 *component parts*) that recur in many characters. Some of these component parts serve as the radical in the character in which they occur, and some do not. Write each character next to a component part that it includes. You may use a character more than once.

特　屋　饺　等　房　趣　白　爱　件　周　爸　旁
数　最　放　宿　唱　得　欢　难　慢　校　间　谁

Shared part	Characters
寸	
土	
方	
亻	
白	
父	
日	

Shared part	Characters
又	
隹	
女	

4.   Reading for basic information

We have learned all of the words, but not all of the characters, in the following passage. Complete the tasks that follow the passage and you will understand the basic information that it contains.

我跟我妹妹睡在一个房间。我们差不多高，所以我买的衣服、鞋子她都可以穿。她又聪明又漂亮，对我也很好，就是不喜欢收拾房间，穿了我的衣服也不放回去。我们的地上都是东西，没有地方走路，因为她常常把穿过的衣服、看完的书、没吃完的东西都扔在地上。洗好的衣服放在椅子上，也不放回柜子里。昨天她穿了我的球鞋，回来以后，臭袜子就放在球鞋里也不洗。今天早上我想穿我那件红色的衬衫，可是找了半天也没找到。最后穿好衣服要出去，看见房间又脏又乱，我很不高兴！我告诉她：我回来以前她最好找到我的红衬衫，把房间收拾好！如果她不收拾房间，不把衣服收起来，不把地扫干净，不把书放回书架上，我以后就不让她穿我的衣服和鞋子！

Your tasks:

a. Find these phrases and circle them:

放回去,

看完

吃完

洗好

收拾好

b. Take a guess:

   1. What do you think 完 means in the phrases 看完的书 and 没吃完的东西? Why?

   2. What do you think 衣服 means in the phrase 洗好的衣服? Why?

   3. What do you think 收拾 means in the phrase 把房间收拾好？ Why?

c. What does my little sister not <u>like</u> to do? Find the answer and put a star next to it.

d. What does my little sister not <u>put away</u>? Find the answer and put a box around it.

e. The narrator says there is no place to walk in their room. Why? Find the answer and underline it.

f. What couldn't the narrator find this morning? Find the answer and put a double underline beneath it.

g. Based on your answers to the previous questions, what do you think this passage is about?

5. Dictionary skills

Following the instructions in Lesson 17 of the textbook, look up these characters in a Chinese dictionary and provide the following information:

a. 完

pronunciation:

meaning:

one two-character word or phrase in which it occurs:

b. 穿

pronunciation:

meaning:

one two-character word or phrase in which it occurs:

c. 衣

pronunciation:

meaning:

one two-character word or phrase in which it occurs:

6. Proofread 大为's email

大为 has written this email to his parents, but he has typed 10 characters wrong. Read the passage aloud, circle the mistakes, and correct them on the answer sheet below.

> 我这级天非常忙，没友时问去买可本。今天非去不可了，因为明天九要开始上课了。一吃 **wán** 早饭，我就到书点去买书了。别的书都卖到了，就是中问课的书卖 **wán** 了，因为洗中文课的学生恨多。

1.	2.	3.	4.	5.
6.	7.	8.	9.	10.

7.   Scrambled sentences

Rewrite these phrases as sentences, putting the words in the correct order to match the English translations.

a. 课本/同屋/我的/的 / 都/在 / 他床 /下边/的

My roommate's textbooks are all under his bed.

b. 但是/想 / 虽然/饺子/很 / 我/吃 / 喜欢/不 / 我/饭馆/吃 /去

Although I really like to eat dumplings, I don't want to go to a restaurant to eat them.

c. chènshān/洗/ gānjìng/容易/ 白色/那件/不 / 的

It's not easy to wash that white shirt clean.

d. 都/在宿舍/每个/一起/里 / 玩电脑/我/ 周末/ 跟室友

Every weekend my roommate and I play (games) on my computer in the dorm.

e. bǎ/放 / 门/请 / 球xié/外边/你的 /在 /

Please put your sneakers outside of the door.

8.   Translation practice

Translate the following passage into English.

小文没有同屋，她一个人住。她的宿舍不大，但是很 gānjìng。房间里的东西不多，一张床、一个 guì 子、一个书 jià、一张 zhuō 子和两 bǎ yǐ子。Zhuō 子上有书、bǐ、liàn 习本，还有一个电脑。

9.   Typing practice

Type the following sentences in Chinese characters and translate them into English.

a. Jīntiān suīrán shì xīngqīliù, bù yòng qù shàng kè, kěshì Měilì qǐ chuáng qǐ de hěn zǎo.

b. Tā yào gēn tā èr niánjí de jǐ ge péngyou yīqǐ qù tā Zhōngguó tóngwū de jiā.

c. Dǎ qiú yǐhòu wǒ tèbié xǐhuān hē bái niúnǎi.

Focus on structure

1.   She's been doing it a long time (Use and structure 19.1)

The following is a list of the things that 美丽 has done and the amount of time she has spent on each activity. Write a sentence in Mandarin for each activity describing how long she has done each activity.

a. *washed clothing*: more than a half hour

b. *played on the computer*: more than three hours

c. *studied Chinese*: more than a year

d. *slept*: more than eight hours

2.   Bird watching (Use and structure 19.2)

谢国强 has a new hobby: bird watching. He is keeping a list of birds that can be seen in and around Beijing, and he checks off birds as he sees them. Write a sentence for each bird, saying whether he has seen it or not. The resultative verb that you will use in each sentence is 看到.

bird	sighted
a. golden oriole (jīn yīng)	
b. egret (白鹭)	✓
c. woodpecker （zhuó mù niǎo）	
d. spotted turtle dove (bān jiū)	✓

a. _____

b. _____

c. _____

d. _____

3.   Have you completed the task? (Use and structure 19.2)

Here are tasks that 国强 has been engaged in. Ask him in complete sentences in Mandarin if he has reached the indicated conclusion or result, as in the example.

Example: 看书 – finished reading → 你看 wán 书了吗？ *or* 你看 wán 书了没有？

a. 找他的手机 – found it →

b. 买电 yǐng piào – bought it →

c. shōushi 房间 – finished (and it is now presentable for his guests) →

d. 写功课 – finished →

e. 选课 – finished →

4. Done! (Use and structure 19.2)

国强 has completed all of the tasks. Answer *yes* to each of the five questions in Exercise 3 above in a complete sentence in Mandarin.

a. _____

b. _____

c. _____

d. _____

e. _____

5. When did he do it? (Use and structure 19.2)

国强 finished some of these tasks a while ago, and some of them just a moment ago. For a few of the tasks, he's almost done. Take your answers in Exercise 4 above and rewrite them, adding in the time adverb in the appropriate location. Then translate each of your responses into English.

a. 刚

b. 早就

c. 现在

d. 刚

e. 早就

6. Not yet done! (Use and stucture 19.2, 19.4)

Here are activities that 小文 has been doing, followed by the result or conclusion that she wants to reach. Write a sentence for each of these activities saying that she has been doing it for a long time but she's still not done.

a. shōushi房间 . . . shōushi gānjìng

b. 做功课 . . . 做wán

c. 找她的手机 。。。 找到

d. 看书。。。 看wán

7.   All except for this (Use and structure 19.5)

Chén 明 is getting his dorm ready for a party. For every part of the preparation, he has only one more thing to do. The following is his list of tasks and remaining activities.

Complete each sentence in Mandarin and then translate the entire sentence into English. Use the expression 就是 *only, it is only, just* in each of your Chinese sentences.

a. 功课都做好了。 *I only haven't finished reviewing the Chinese characters.*

   Mandarin:

   English:

b. 我 bǎ 房间 shōushi 好了。 *I just haven't put the books back in the bookcase.*

   Mandarin:

   English:

c. 吃的，喝的都买好了。 *I only haven't bought the beer.*

   Mandarin:

   English:

d. 我已经给同学 fā 了duǎnxìn 请他们来。*I just haven't invited my teachers.*

   Mandarin:

   English:

e. 别的都好了。 *We just haven't selected the music.*

   Mandarin:

   English:

8.   What do they do before the party? (Use and structure 18.11, 19.2)

Chén 明 and his friends are all going to be busy before the party. Here is what they are doing. Translate their activities into English.

a. 在 Chén 明的同学来以前他得先 bǎ 汉字 fù 习 wán。

b. 在美丽去 Chén 明家以前，她先给**爸爸**妈妈打电话。

c. 在大为去晚会以前，他得先接小文和美丽。

d. 在王 Màikè 去 Chén 明那儿以前，他先帮 Chén 明买几 píng 可乐。

9.   *Both* AdjV₁ *and* AdjV₂ (Use and structure 19.7)

Here are comments and observations that **Chén** 明's guests make during the party. Write them in complete sentences in Mandarin using **yòu** AdjV₁ **yòu** AdjV₂.

a. **Chén** 明的宿舍 (piàoliang, gānjìng)

b. cài (多，好吃)

c. 水果 (好看，好吃)

10.   Have to do it? No need to do it? (Use and structure 19.9, 19.10)

The following is a list of activities on 美丽's "to do" list. She has put * next to all of the activities she absolutely has to do today, and she has put ☺ next to all of the activities she need not do today. Write a Mandarin sentence for each activity saying that she has to do it (非 . . . 不可) or need not do it (不用). If the verb phrase consists of a verb + object, state the object before 非 . . . 不可.

我今天:

a. review Chinese *

b. go to the library ☺

c. finish reading the economics textbook ☺

d. clean up the room *

e. buy a pair of sneakers *

f. go online to find a subway map ☺

11.   Translation challenge

Translate these sentences into Mandarin, using the phrase(s) and structure(s) provided.

a. Take your smelly sneakers and put them outside the room. (bǎ)

b. You've got so many things on your bed. No wonder you can't sleep. (难 guài)

c. You've already been doing your homework for more than three hours. Do you mean to say you haven't finished yet? (已经, 难道, resultative verb)

d. That computer is really expensive. No wonder your parents won't buy it for you! (jí 了, 难 guài)

e. This milk smells bad. You have to throw it out. (非 . . . 不可)

f. The new semester starts tomorrow. You have to finish selecting classes tonight. (非 . . . 不可)

Focus on communication

> Additional Focus on communication exercises as well as classroom activities for spoken communication are on the Teachers' Resource website.

1. What do you say?

What do you say in each of the following situations? *Type* your answers, using characters where we have learned them.

a. You are mad that your younger brother messes up your room. Ask him to straighten it up before you come back tonight.

b. You are in a hurry to leave. Ask your sister nicely if she can help you put away all the clothes you threw on the bed.

c. You walk into the room and wonder what smells so bad! Ask your roommate to hurry up (more quickly) and open the windows.

d. You proudly tell your friend about the bargain you had: you bought a pair of shoes and two white shirts and only spent $15.00.

e. You wonder if your roommate has seen the pair of pants you purchased yesterday. You've been looking for them for a long time.

f. While cleaning out the refrigerator, tell your roommate that this sandwich has been there over a week, (and) he has to throw it away. (In other words, he must throw it away!)

g. It's been two weeks since school began. Your teacher realized you didn't buy a textbook. No wonder you did poorly on your character quiz! What does the teacher say?

h. You are checking out a potential apartment room for rent. You don't like it because it's small and expensive. You don't have a place to put your clothes.

i. You ask if your roommate can sweep the floor clean because you are busy putting books back on the shelf.

j. You are invited to a St. Patrick's Day party where you are supposed to wear green. You look at your closet and complain that you have blue, black, white, and red clothes. You just don't have a green shirt. What should you do?

k. You brought home from school a bag of dirty clothes. Ask your mom if she can wash them clean for you.

2. Mini-dialogues (Use and structure 19.3, 19.7, 19.8, 19.10

Complete each dialogue by using the structure in parentheses.

a. A: 你不是去买 xié 吗？怎么没买到？

   B: 那些 xié _____, 我都不喜欢。(yòu . . . yòu . . .)

b. A: 你打suan什么时候开始写 功课？

　　B: 我＿＿＿＿＿＿＿＿＿＿＿＿＿＿＿＿＿＿＿＿＿＿＿。(一 ... 就 ...)

c. A: 你看见我的日文课本了吗？我已经找了半天了。

　　B: 没看见。我＿＿＿＿＿＿＿＿＿＿＿＿＿＿＿＿＿就来 bāng你找。(bǎ)

d. A: 你看，这是我昨天买的yīfu, 你觉得怎么样？

　　B: ＿＿＿＿＿＿＿＿＿＿＿＿＿＿＿＿＿! 多少钱？我也想买一jiàn！ (jí 了)

e. A: ＿＿＿＿＿＿＿＿＿＿＿＿＿＿＿＿＿? (不bì)

　　B: 你怎么 wàng 了？今天是 Veteran's Day, 放一天jià。

3. Before and after (Use and structure 19.2, 19.8, 19.11)

Here are pictures of 谢为中's room, before and after he cleaned it up.

BEFORE   **AFTER**

Part I. Look at the BEFORE picture. Translate each of the following questions into Mandarin and answer them in Mandarin:

a. What is in the closet?

　　Q: ＿＿＿＿＿＿＿＿＿＿＿＿＿＿＿＿＿＿＿?

　　A: ＿＿＿＿＿＿＿＿＿＿＿＿＿＿＿＿＿＿＿

b. Where is Xie Weizhong's computer?

　　Q: ＿＿＿＿＿＿＿＿＿＿＿＿＿＿＿＿＿＿＿?

　　A: ＿＿＿＿＿＿＿＿＿＿＿＿＿＿＿＿＿＿＿

c. Where are all the books?

　　Q: ＿＿＿＿＿＿＿＿＿＿＿＿＿＿＿＿＿＿＿?

　　A: ＿＿＿＿＿＿＿＿＿＿＿＿＿＿＿＿＿＿＿

d. What's on the floor?

    Q: _____?

    A: _____

e. How many pencils are there in Xie Weizhong's room? Where are they?

    Q: _____?

    A: _____

Part II. Look at the BEFORE picture and decide whether the following statements are true or false. If a statement is false, please correct it. For example,

Guì子里有很多xié. → *False*: Guì子里<u>没有 xié</u>.

( ) a. 谢为中的电 nǎo 在床下边。

( ) b. 床上有 xié, yīfu 还有电 nǎo。

( ) c. 谢为中的 bǐ 都在 yǐ 子上。

( ) d. 谢为中的床上有 xié, 地上有 xié, zhuō 子上也有 xié.

( ) e. 谢为中的 guì 子里没有 yīfu.

( ) f. 谢为中的书 jià 上有一 píng 水

Part III. Look at the AFTER picture. Write *at least four* sentences to describe how 谢为中 has cleaned up his room. You need to use "bǎ-structure"：For example: 谢为中 bǎ 水放在书jià上。

a. _____

b. _____

c. _____

d. _____

Part IV. Look at the AFTER picture and write a few sentences to answer this question: 请问，你觉得谢为中 **bǎ** 房间 **shōushi** 好了吗？为什么？

_____

_____

_____

4. A conversation (Use and structure 19.2, 19.5, 19.7, 19.10)

Part I. Complete this conversation between Mǎ Xiǎowén and her mother by filling in each blank with a word from the following list.

只是	**wán**	不 **bì**	多	没
因为	就是	的	**yòu**	开

马太太：小文，昨天晚上我给你打电话你怎么不在？

小文： 妈，昨天大为和国强在他们的宿舍_____晚会，我们都去了。

马太太：晚会有意思吗？

小文：有意思，_____，他们的宿舍太小，去的人太多，没有 yǐ 子坐。

马太太：你们吃什么？

小文：国强做了很多吃的，很多东西都_____吃 wán。我 dài 了一些饺子回来。

马太太：小文，开学已经一个_____星期了，忙不忙？

小文：还好。我的课选好了，课本也买好了，_____宿舍还没有 shōushi 好。

马太太： 没关系，慢慢 shōushi. 这个 周末回家吃饭吧！我打 suàn 做你最喜欢 _____红 shāo ròu.

小文：这个周末不行，_____我下个星期有考试。下个周末吧！我一考_____试就回家。

马太太：要不要爸爸去学校 接你？

小文：_____，坐地 tiě_____快 yòu piányi。

马太太：那也好。那下个星期六见。

小文：妈，再见。

Part II. Q&A. Read the dialogue above. Then, answer the questions in Mandarin.

a. 昨天晚上小文为什么不在宿舍里？

b. 小文觉得大为和国强的宿舍怎么样？

c. 他们开学多久了？

d. 开学到现在，小文什么事还没有做wán？

e. 这个周末小文会回家吗？为什么？

f. 小文怎么回家？

5. Writing (Use and structure 19.2, 19.3, 19.7, 19.8, 19.9, 19.11)

Look at this picture and imagine what this mother is saying to her son right now. Use the following structure/words in your paragraph:

luàn	非 . . . 不可	**yòu . . . yòu . . .**	**shōushi**	**bǎ**

Lesson 20 看 bìng
Getting sick and seeing a doctor

Listening comprehension exercises, structure drills for listening and speaking practice, audio files for vocabulary, and the sentence pyramids are on the companion website.

Focus on literacy

Additional exercises focusing on Chinese characters are on the companion website.

1. First two strokes

Consult the stroke order flow chart in the textbook and write the first **two** strokes of each of the following characters.

a. 菜   f. 服

b. 片   g. 发

c. 睡   h. 院

d. 头   i. 穿

e. 带   j. 让

2. Radicals

a. The following are characters that we have learned through this lesson. Rewrite each character in the row next to its radical.

酒	能	菜	像	作	活	冷	件	花
挣	服	把	济	净	打	期	脑	决

月	
廿	
氵	
亻	
扌	
冫	

b. For some of these characters, the radical helps to identify the meaning of the character. Circle all of the characters for which this is the case. How is the meaning of the radical in each of these characters related to meaning of the character in which it occurs? Consult the *Focus on Radicals* file for Lesson 20 on the companion website as you do this exercise.

3.   Find the bùjiàn (部件 component parts)

The following are characters introduced in this and previous lessons along with a list of **bùjiàn** (部件 *component parts*) that recur in many characters. Some of these component parts serve as the radical in the character in which they occur, and some do not. Write each character next to a component part that it includes. You may use a character more than once.

快　发　院　把　决　爸　块　友　园　服　数　最
右　坏　有　奶　脑　菜　帮　还　元　带　把　爱

Shared part	Characters
夬	
ナ	
巴	
又	
元	
女	
月	
不	
米	
巾	

4. Look for the rhymes

The following is a list of characters that you have learned. Pair each character with another on the list that rhymes or nearly rhymes with it and shares a shēngpáng (声旁) "phonetic element."

把　先　店　钟　很　又　爸　话　百　上　如

妈　白　活　友　女　让　点　选　中　跟　码

5. Reading comprehension I

Read the paragraph and see what happens to 大为 after the Lesson 20 text. Answer the first question in English and the remaining questions in Mandarin.

从yī院回来以后，我还是觉得很累，所以决定今天在家xiūxi。换了睡衣我就上床睡觉了。不知道睡了多久，国强从学校回来了，还带了小文来看我。小文一看见我就说：你的ěrduo怎么这么红？一定是屋子里太rè。她把chuānghù打开，给了我一bēi水。我睡了好几个钟头，还吃了yī生给的yào，觉得shū服多了。晚上小文买了饺子，还做了jī tāng。吃饭的时候她要我小心一点，不要一次吃太多。我想明天早上起床以后如果头不yūn, dù子也不téng了，我就会去学校。

a. What do you think "睡衣" is? Why?

b. Did Dàwéi go to school today? How did you know? Cite your evidence.

c. Why did Xiǎowén open the window?

d. Is Dàwéi feeling better now? What has contributed to his recovery?

e. Did Xiǎowén stay for dinner? How do you know?

f. Is Dàwéi going to school tomorrow?

6.   Reading comprehension II

Read the passage and

- locate the section of the text that provides the answer to each of these questions by writing in the question number next to the text.
- answer the questions in Mandarin.

Note: **yòu + action verb + 了** means to *do an action again that was done in the past.*

我的朋友李明非常喜欢学校 páng 边的中国饭馆。他每次去都吃他最喜欢的红 shāo ròu。昨天他 yòu 跟朋友一起去了那家中国饭馆。他的朋友说你已经吃了好几次红 shāo ròu 了。今天别吃了。吃别的菜吧。他没有吃红 shāo ròu，吃了几个比 jiào là 的菜，还喝了一点啤酒。吃 wán 饭他的 dù 子就不 shū 服，晚上睡不着觉，也上了好几次cè所。早上一起床就想 tù。他以为是因为饭菜不干净,可是他的室友说chú 了他以外别人都没事. 大 gài 是因为 他不习惯吃là 的，李明决定下次只能吃红 shāo ròu 了。

a. Where is the restaurant that Li Ming likes?

b. When did he most recently go to that restaurant?

c. Using 是 . . . 的 – who did he go to the restaurant with?

d. Did he order 红 shāo ròu? Why or why not?

e. When did Li Ming begin to feel sick?

f. What does Li Ming think is the cause of his illness?

g. Is he correct? Why or why not?

h. Why did Li Ming probably get sick?

i. What do you think Li Ming should do the next time he goes to that restaurant?

7.   Dictionary skills

a. Following the instructions in Lesson 17 of the textbook, look up the following characters in a Chinese dictionary and indicate their pronunciation and meaning.

吐

肚

b. What component part do the characters 吐 and 肚 share? Write it here: _____.

It is a character on its own. Look it up in a dictionary to find its pronunciation and write it here: _____. What information does it provide in the characters 吐 and 肚?

8. Proofread 大为's email

大为 has written this email to a friend back home, but he has typed 12 different characters wrong (some more than once). Read the passage aloud, circle the mistakes, and correct them on the answer sheet below. If the same mistake occurs twice, count it as a single mistake.

这个兴起学小的店yǐng　　院有"家"这个店yǐng。我没看过，不只到这个电yǐng　　好坏。我文我的同屋看过每有。他说他看过，他很习欢，以经看了好九次了。他还说他可一跟我在看一次。

1.	2.	3.	4.	5.	6.	7.
8.	9.	10.	11.	12.		

9. Scrambled sentences

Rewrite these phrases as sentences, putting the words in the correct order to match the English translations.

a. 东西/床 / 在/别 / 把 /的/放 / 我的/ 上/你

Don't put your things on my bed.

b. 饭馆/吧 / 去/那 / 吃/ 我们/下次/家 / 饭

Let's go to that restaurant to eat next time.

c. 酒/喜欢/为什么/喝 / 中国人/红

Why do Chinese people like to drink red wine?

d. 可能/不 / 觉得/吃 / 你/太 / 你/会 / 得/shū服 /如果 /快

If you eat too fast, you may feel uncomfortable.

e. là的/你 / 习惯/好像/不 / 吃

It seems that you are not used to eating spicy things.

10. Translation practice

Translate the following passage into English.

王明有女朋友。他们是一年级在一个学生晚会认识的。她是去年从英国来的。她也是来中国学中文的。她来中国以前在英国的时候就开始学中文了。她说中文说得非常好。在那个晚会上他们一起唱歌、tiào wǔ、说了很多话、也吃了很多东西。晚上很晚才回宿舍。

11. Typing practice

Type the following sentences in Chinese characters and translate them into English. Be sure to proofread your typed sentences!

a. Wǒ bù xíguàn yòng kuàizi (筷子 chopsticks) chī Zhōngguó fàn.

b. Nǐ de sùshè zěnme zhème gānjìng!

c. Nǐ fā shāo le. Jīntiān bù shàng kè ba.

d. Shuì jiào yǐqián bié hē jiǔ.

e. Wǒ de tóngwū yǐjing shuì le shí gè zhōngtóu le.

Focus on structure

1. How many times? (Use and structure 20.2)

The following is a list of activities that 小文 has done this week and the number of times she has done each one. Rewrite this information in complete Mandarin sentences, using characters where we have learned them.

a. eaten Sichuan food (twice)

b. cleaned her room (once)

c. washed clothes (three times)

d. drunk beer (once)

e. seen the doctor (*had an illness*) (twice)

2. 还是 and huòzhě (Use and structure 20.5)

Translate these sentences into Mandarin, using 还是 or **huòzhě** in each sentence as appropriate.

a. Would you like to drink coffee or tea?

b. Tonight we can watch television or listen to music.

c. You can go see a doctor tonight or tomorrow morning.

d. Do you prefer to bathe at night or in the morning?

e. Are you going to major in Chinese or Japanese?

3.   Resultative verbs in the potential form (Use and structure 19.2, 20.6)
Translate each of the following sentences into English.

a. 我打不开这个门。

b. 今天晚上的功课太多了。我做不wán。

c. 这jiàn yī服太zāng 了。我洗不干净。

d. 老师说话说得那么快，你听得懂吗？

e. Hànbǎo (hamburgers) 在中国吃得到吗？

f. 明天是我的生日。今天晚上一定睡不 zháo。

g. 这个字写得太小了。我看不见是哪个字。

h. 我找不到那个电 yǐng 院。请告诉我怎么走。

4.   Details of a past event (Use and structure 20.9)
Guoqiang's father is asking him about his activities last weekend. Express each question in Mandarin, using 是。。。的 in each question.

a. What day did you eat in a restaurant?

b. Who did you have dinner with?

c. Where did you eat?

d. What time did you return to the dorm?

e. What time did you go to sleep?

5.   Your personal information (Use and structure 20.9)

Answer questions (a)–(d) truthfully in Mandarin, using 是。。。的 in each sentence.

a. Where were you born?

b. What month and date were you born?

c. What year were you born?

d. When did you begin to study Chinese?

Translate (e)–(f) into Mandarin.

e. When did you graduate high school?

f. When did you select your major?

6.   Chú 了 . . . 以外 (Use and structure 20.10)

Rewrite each sentence using the structure **chú** 了 . . . 以外, as in the example, and translate your new sentences into English.

Example:

我喜欢吃中国菜，也喜欢吃美国菜→ Chú 了中国菜以外，我也喜欢吃美国菜。

a. 我妈妈会做中国菜，也会做法国菜→

   Mandarin:

   English:

b. 我发 shāo，头也很 téng →

   Mandarin:

   English:

c. 地上有衣服，地上也有书→

   Mandarin:

   English:

d. 我选了 几门 zhuānyè 课和一门音乐课→

   Mandarin:

   English:

e. 他每天都忙 zhe 工作和学习→

   Mandarin:

   English:

f. 我喜欢唱歌，我朋友都喜欢唱歌→

7.   Translation challenge 1

Translate these sentences into English.

a. 我今天一天忙 zhe fù 习功课，因为明天我有三个考试。

b. Chú 了我以外，小文也没 cānjiā 今天早上的考试。我们都起晚了。

c. Chú 了 dù 子不 shū 服以外，我不发 shāo，头也不 téng。可能是昨天晚上吃得太多了。

d. 今天的中文功课太多了，吃晚饭以前做不 wán。

e. 因为我对中国很有兴趣，所以下个学期我要选一门中国文 huà huòzhě 中国经济的课。

f. 我带他到学校的 yī 院看 bìng。Yī 生说他不习惯吃 là 的，所以 dù 子 téng，很快就会好，还给他开 yào 了。

g. 这个电 yǐng 我很喜欢，已经看了三次了。

h. 美丽学汉字学得很快，也学得很好。她每天把 xīn 的汉字都写三次。

8.   Translation challenge 2

Translate these sentences into Mandarin.

a. I was sick all day yesterday and didn't finish my homework.

b. You ate too much. Next time don't eat so much.

c. This is my first time eating spicy food.

d. Q: When you traveled in China, could you understand people?

   A: Except for Sichuan people, I understood everyone.

e. I finished reading that book but I didn't understand it.

f. Where did the two of you meet?

g. I'm not interested in music. Whenever I listen to music, I fall asleep.

Focus on communication

Additional Focus on communication exercises as well as classroom activities for spoken communication are on the Teachers' Resource website.

1.   What do you say?

What do you say in each of the following situations? Type your answers, using characters where we have learned them.

a. Your roommate looks sick to you. You want to know what's going on.

b. You complain about your sleep problem: you wake up several times in the middle of night.

c. You wonder when your friend started driving because he doesn't seem to be a very experienced driver.

d. You complain about a headache, an upset stomach, and nausea.

e. You need to explain your symptoms to the doctor: you have a fever and have been coughing and sneezing since last week.

f. You want to let your friend know that you might arrive late, either 3 p.m. or 3:30 p.m.

g. You are telling the hostess that you're too full to eat anything when she insists that you get a second helping of the food.

h. Your little brother has a runny nose and keeps sneezing. Tell him that the weather is getting cold, to wear more clothes, and to be careful to not catch a cold.

i. (You are a doctor) After hearing the patient describe her runny nose, ask what other symptoms she has.

2.   大家都 bìng 了 (Use and structure 20.11)

It's the flu season and everyone in Zhāng Guóshēng's class is sick. Use the information in the pictures to complete each sentence below. Then translate the sentences into English.

谢朋

张国生

钱大同

常有文

高南

毛爱丽

李思思

a. _____fā烧了， shēntǐ 很不 shū 服。

English:

b. _____ bìng 了 好几天了，都没有来上课。

English:

c. _____可能是吃坏 dù 子了。昨天一天 lā 了好几次 dù 子。

English:

d. _____这几天一起床就一直 késou。

English:

e. _____头很 téng，吃了 yào 也没有用。

English:

f. _____dù 子 téng, 想tù, 吃不下 。

English:

g. _____去看 yī 生。Yī 生看了她的 sǎng 子说她 yīnggāi 是 gǎnmào 了

English:

3.   Mini-dialogues (Use and structure 20.5, 20.10)

Use the structure in the parentheses to complete each mini-dialogue.

a. A: 你说这个学期你选了中文课，还有呢？

   B: _____。(chú 了 . . .
   以外)

b. A: 你周末 做什么？

   B: 我常常 _____。（huòzhě）

c. A: 今天回家请写 dì 五课、dì 六课的功课，明天给我。

   B: 老师，功课太多了，我_____! (Verb 得/不 + resultative
   ending)

d. A: 吃中国饭你怎么不用 kuài 子？

   B: _____。 (不习惯)

e. A: 明天是你生日，我们去那家日本饭馆吃饭吧!

   B: 换一家好不好，那家饭馆我_____。(好几次)

4.   Meet your new teammates (Use and structure 20.9)

You will be participating in a three-week volunteer program in China during the break. Today is the orientation, and you are meeting the other team members for the first time.

Part I. Write down the questions that you can ask your teammates. Use 是 . . . 的 in your questions for (a), (b), and (d).

Example:

Where are you from?: 你是从哪儿来的？

a. Whom did you come with?

   _____

b. When did you begin to study Chinese?

   _____

c. How did you hear about this job?

   _____

d. How did you get here today?

   _____

e. Why do you want to go to China?

   _____

f. *Write at least one more question:*

_____

_____

Part II. Below is information about four other volunteers. Translate the questions into Mandarin and answer them in Mandarin.

	Country	What year did they begin studying Chinese?	Where did they learn Chinese?	Whom did they come here with?
Zhēnní	France	Two years ago	Paris (Bālí)	Alone
Tāngmǔ	US	Last September	College	One classmate
Jiékè	UK	This summer	Beijing	Two friends
Mòlì	Japan	Last month	Tokyo	Her older sister

a. Who came here with her older sister?

Question:

Answer:

b. Where is Tāngmǔ from?

Question:

Answer:

c. Did Jiékè study Chinese in Tokyo?

Question:

Answer:

d. How long has Zhēnní been learning Chinese?

Question:

Answer:

Part III. It's your turn to introduce yourself. Write at least four sentences about yourself.

_____

_____

_____

_____

_____

_____

5. Writing: 小王 is not feeling well

Part I. This is a story about 小王. Rearrange the sentences in the right order to form a cohesive paragraph.

a. 虽然没有 lā dù 子，可是，头一 zhí 很 téng， dù 子也不太 shū 服。

b. 从饭馆回来以后我有点儿不 shū 服，就去睡觉了。

c. 早上我的同 wū 说我大 gài 喝太多酒了。

d. Yè 里睡不 zháo，起来好几次。

e. 我下午三点才吃午饭，所以晚饭吃得不多。

f. 我吃了 yào 就觉得好一点了。

g. 昨天晚上大为请我们几个人去一家 xīn 开的饭馆吃饭，因为他找到工作 了。

h. 他给了我一 片头 téng yào，还叫我多喝一点 茶。

i. 不过因为太高兴，喝了好几 瓶 pí 酒。

Part II. Below is a dialogue between 小王 and his roommate. Fill in the roommate's part based on the paragraph in Part I.

同屋：

小王：我昨天晚上没睡好， 头 **téng jí** 了。

同屋：

小王：我 **dù** 子也不太 **shū**服。

同屋：

小王：昨天吃了晚饭以后就开始不 **shū** 服。

同屋：

小王：我是在一家 **xīn** 开的饭馆吃的晚饭。

同屋：

小王：我吃得不多，就喝了三 **píng pí** 酒。

同屋：

小王：喝太多了？那怎么 **bàn** 呢？

同屋：

小王：谢谢。我现在就吃。

Part III. 小王 is feeling sick this morning so he missed his class today. Help him write an email message to his Chinese teacher apologizing for skipping the class today. He needs to explain why he missed the class.

李老师，您好：

我是您二年级中文课的学生。对不起，_____

_____

_____

_____

_____

_____

明天如果您有时间，我可以去找您问几个问题吗？谢谢！

王明明

Lesson 21 天气和气候变化
Weather and climate change

🎧 Listening and speaking

Listening comprehension exercises, structure drills for listening and speaking practice, audio files for vocabulary, and the sentence pyramids are on the companion website.

Focus on literacy

Additional exercises focusing on Chinese characters are on the companion website.

1. First two strokes

Consult the stroke order flow chart in the textbook and write the first **two** strokes of each of the following characters.

a. 热

b. 亮

c. 零

d. 将

e. 夏

f. 脏

g. 加

h. 化

i. 病

j. 照

2. Radicals

a. The following are characters that we have learned through this lesson. Rewrite each character in the row next to its radical.

照	环	该	坏	概	床	校	酒	热
海	境	济	末	流	让	漂	活	理

氵	
灬	
土	
王	
讠	
木	

b. For some of these characters, the radical helps to identify the meaning of the character. Circle all of the characters for which this is the case. How is the meaning of the radical in each of these characters related to the meaning of the character in which it occurs? Consult the *Focus on Radicals* file for Lesson 21 on the companion website as you do this exercise.

3.　Find the bùjiàn (部件 component parts)

The following are characters introduced in this and previous lessons along with a list of **bùjiàn** (部件 *component parts*) that recur in many characters. Some of these component parts serve as the radical in the character in which they occur, and some do not. Write each character next to a component part that it includes. You may use a character more than once.

岁　汉　校　周　没　麻　发　变　脏　较　床
最　爱　对　果　饺　慢　多　外　在　坐　名

Shared part	**Characters**
夕	
交	
木	
又	
土	
日	

4.　Look for the rhymes

The following is a list of characters that you have learned. Pair each character with another on the list that rhymes or nearly rhymes with it and shares a shēngpáng (声旁) "phonetic element."

活　较　房　点　饺　咖　漂　昨　该　方　远　孩
院　玩　长　作　张　店　校　话　加　票　放

交	
票	
乍	
方	
元	
长	
占	
加	
舌	
亥	

5. Reading for basic information

We have learned all of the words, but not all of the characters, in the following passage. Complete the tasks that follow the passage and you will comprehend most if not all of it.

有的人常常把下雪想得很漂亮，房子上是雪、路上也是雪。我想这些人大概没有看见过下雪。第一，下雪的时候常常很冷。天气太冷让人觉得很不舒服。第二，下雪以后出去、进来、走路、开车都很不方便。第三，下雪以后，很快路上就很脏，鞋、衣服、汽车都很容易脏。下雪的时候可能很漂亮，但是漂亮的时间不长。我真的不喜欢下雪。

Your tasks:

a. Find and circle the word 雪. How many times does the character 雪 occur in the paragraph?

b. In the first sentence, the narrator indicates two places where can you see 雪. What are they? Indicate where in the paragraph you find the information.

c. This paragraph contrasts two perspectives on 雪. Whose perspectives are they?

A: B:

What does A think about 雪? Put a box around the words that indicate this.

d. The narrator believes that A's perspective is incorrect. Why? Place a double underline below the sentence that explains why A's perspective is incorrect.

e. Find and circle the words 第一，第二，第三

These words introduce three pieces of evidence that the narrator provides to support his/her point of view. What are the main words in each piece of evidence that indicate the narrator's point of view?

第一:

第二:

第三:

f. We haven't learned the character 第, but the bottom component is identical with another character that we have learned, and it shares the pronunciation with that character. What is that character?

g. In two sentences, explain what this passage is about.

6. Dictionary skills

Following the instructions in Lesson 17 of the textbook, look up these characters in a Chinese dictionary and provide the following information:

a. 便

   pronunciation:

   meaning:

b. 雪

   pronunciation:

   meaning:

7. Proofread 大为's email

大为 continues his email correspondence with his classmates back in the US. He hasn't yet proofread this message, but when he does, he will find that 13 characters are wrong. (One character is written wrong twice.) Read the passage aloud, circle the mistakes, and correct them on the answer sheet below.

作天晚上下 xuě 了。下了一 yè。今天早上我一起床就王 chuānghu 外边看。我觉的很票亮。路上没友很多车，可是人非常都。他们都穿了很多一服。有的人 sǎo xuě，有的人玩 xuě。我跟我的同屋也到外边去 wán xuě。wán 了差不多一个中头。玩得很高兴，可是国一会儿我觉的非常冷。回宿舍我们喝了很多热差、吃了一点东西以后，才觉得书服了。

I.	2.	3.	4	5.	6.
7. & 8.	9.	IO.	II.	I2.	I3.

8.   Scrambled sentences

Rewrite these phrases as sentences, putting the words in the correct order to match the English translations.

a. shū 服/离 /我家/很近/天气/所以/夏天/的 / 特别/海边 /

My home is close the coast, so weather in the summer is particularly comfortable.

b. 的/变好/天气/说/ 天气/会 / yùbào/后天

The weather forecast says that the weather will turn good the day after tomorrow.

c. 穿/管 / 呢 /老师/要 / 我/衣服/为什么/什么

Why does the teacher care what clothing I wear?

9.   Typing practice

Type the following sentences in Chinese characters and translate them into English. You can type the word in parentheses in pinyin. Be sure to proofread your typed sentences!

a. Tā de yīfu dōu hěn piàoliang, wǒ xiǎng yīdìng yě dōu hěn guì.

b. Zhège xuéqī nǐ yīnggāi xuǎn yī mén Zhōngguó wénhuà kè.

c. Wǒ de sùshè hěn (shū)fu, zhǐ shì yǒu yīdiǎn zāng.

Focus on structure

1.   Getting more and more . . . (Use and structure 21.1)

Describe each situation in a complete sentence that includes **yuè**来**yuè**, as in the example. Note: 前年 *the year before last year (2 years ago)*

Example:

Wind speed:

9 a.m.: 5 miles/hour, 10 a.m.: 10 miles/hour, 11 a.m.: 20 miles/hour

Your description: **Fēng yuè**来**yuè** 大。

a. Median home price in the US:

前年	去年	今年
$250,000	$300,000	$350,000

your description: _____

b. 天 qì yùbào 说 (this week's weather):

| 今天：80°F | 明天：85°F | 后天：90°F |

your description: _____

c. 北京的 dōng 天 (average temperature):

| 前年: –5°C | 去年: –6°C | 今年: –7°C |

your description: _____

d. 张小弟：

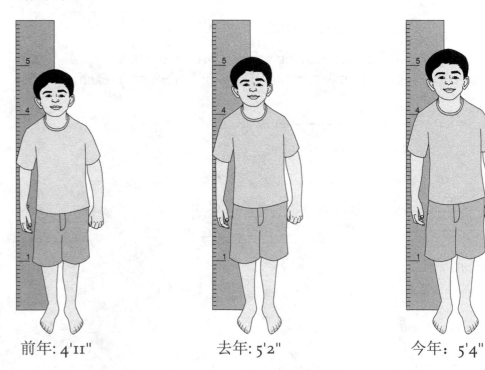

前年: 4'11"   去年: 5'2"   今年: 5'4"

your description: _____

2. Winter brings changes (Use and structure 21.7)

Translate these sentences into English to see what happens in the winter.

Dōng天到了，_____

a. 天气变冷了.

b. 日子 *(days)* 变 **duǎn** 了。

c. 路上的人变少了。

d. 大家穿的衣服变多了。

3.   Become more and more . . . (Use and structure 21.1)

Answer each question in a complete sentence that includes the phrase **yuè** 来 **yuè**.

a. 你觉得今年的中文考试怎么样？

_____

b. 全球 **nuǎn** 化是什么？

_____

c. 如果你没有时间 **shōushí** 房间，你的房间可能会怎么样？

_____

4.   Unable to do it, Part I (Use and structure 21.4)

Complete each sentence by adding the missing information to match the English translations and complete the English translation for (a). Use **V**不了 once in each sentence.

a. 今年的夏天真热，我快_____了。

_____, *I almost can't stand it.*

b. **Màikè** 的功课太多了。他_____今天的晚会。

Maike has too much homework. He can't go to tonight's party.

c. *The bookstore is not open.* 我们_____书了。

We can't buy books.

d. 我_____她的名字。

I am unable to forget her name.

5.   Unable to do it, Part II (Use and structure 21.4)

Fill in the blank with an appropriate **V-**不了 **(V bùliǎo)** expression to complete each sentence to match the English translation.

去不了   走不了   上不了   晚不了   来不了

a. 我现在还有一点事，_____ 。你们别等我了，先走吧。

I have something to do now and cannot leave. Don't wait for me. Go on ahead.

b. 对不起，这个星期天我得回家。我_____了你家。

Sorry, I have to go home this Sunday. I can't go to your home.

c. 国强给我打电话说他今天晚上得去工作，_____了。

Guoqiang phoned me and said that he has to go to work tonight and he cannot come (here).

d. 电 **yǐng** 八点开始。现在才六点半。我们_____。

The movie starts at 8. It's only 6:30 right now. We won't be late.

e. 我有点不 **shū** 服。请你告诉老师今天的课我_____了。

I'm not feeling well. Please tell the teacher I won't be able to attend today's class.

6.   Two things are the same (Use and structure 21.5)

Answer the following questions in complete Mandarin sentences based on the tables.

Month	Jan	Feb	Mar	Apr	May	Jun	Jul	Aug	Sep	Oct	Nov	Dec
Temperature (Celsius)	–4.6	–2.7	4.5	13.1	19.8	24.4	25.8	24.4	19.4	12.4	4.1	–2.7

a. Which two months are equally cold?

_____

b. Which two months of the year are equally hot?

_____

dì 一件衣服	**dì** 二件衣服	**dì** 三件衣服	**dì** 四件衣服	**dì** 五件衣服
$39.99	$19.99	$9.99	$19.99	$9.99

c. Which two shirts are equally expensive?

_____

d. Which two shirts are the same?

_____

7.   Comparisons (Use and structure 21.8)

Answer each of the following questions in a complete sentence based on the illustration. Use 比 in each of your answers.

a. 谁的**guì** 子 **luàn?** _____

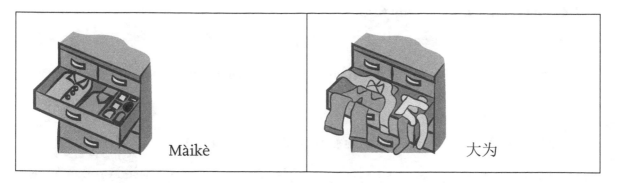

Màikè

大为

b. 谁的房间干净？ _____

关小东

王小真

c. 谁的家近？

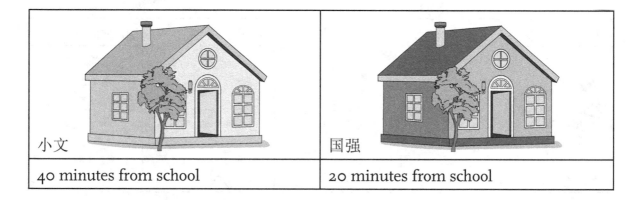

小文	国强
40 minutes from school	20 minutes from school

8.   More comparisons (Use and structure 21.5 and 21.8)

Here are some facts about 高美丽 and her friend 马小文. Answer the following questions in complete Mandarin sentences based on this information.

高美丽	马小文
age: 21 height: 5'4" courses this semester: 4 tests next week: 2 very smart	age: 20 height: 5'5" courses this semester: 5 tests next week: 1 very smart

a. Are 高美丽 and 马小文 the same age? (hint: equally big)

b. Are 高美丽 and 马小文 the same height?

c. Who has more classes this semester? (hint: whose courses are more?)

d. Who has more tests next week?

e. Who is smarter, 高美丽 or 马小文?

9. Asking about comparisons (Use and structure 21.5 and 21.8)

Translate the questions in Exercise 8 above into Mandarin.

a. _____

b. _____

c. _____

d. _____

e. _____

10. Confirm my assumptions (Use and structure 21.6)

Ask the following questions in Mandarin to confirm your assumptions about 高美丽 and 马小文.

a. Isn't it the case that 高美丽 and 马小文 are the same age (*equally big*)?

b. Isn't it the case that 高美丽 and 马小文 are the same height (*equally tall*)?

c. Isn't it the case that 高美丽 is smarter than 马小文?

11. That's the difference between A and B (Use and structure 21.9)

Sum up each of these sentences by saying, "that's the difference between (A) and (B)" as in the example.

Example:

Chūn天常常guā fēng，qiū天不guā fēng。 →

这就是chūn天和qiū天的不同。

a. 美国人喜欢早上洗澡。中国人喜欢晚上洗澡。

b. 北京一年四 jì，南加 zhōu 一年一 jì。

c. 美丽很用功，她的妹妹太喜欢玩。

Focus on communication

> Additional Focus on communication exercises as well as classroom activities for spoken communication are on the Teachers' Resource website.

1.   What do you say?

What do you say in each of the following situations? Type your answers, using characters where we have learned them.

a. Complain about how you can't stand today's high temperatures anymore.

b. Advise your little brother to wear more clothes because it's cold outside.

c. Tell your mother that you're already 21. Of course you know how to clean up your room.

d. At the end of your guests' visit, express your wish for them to come again when they get a chance in the future.

e. You wonder why your Chinese teacher cares about what time you go to bed.

f. You brought some soup to your friend who just had her wisdom tooth removed. Explain that you made the *chicken soup* (jī tāng) because you were afraid that she's unable to eat other food.

g. Comment on the weather in your area these past few days.

h. Explain why you like (or dislike) rain.

i. Compare the winter in your hometown with Beijing's, based on what you read in this lesson.

2.   Mini-dialogues (Use and structure 21.1, 21.4, 21.5, 21.8)

Use the words in parentheses to complete each mini-dialogue.

a. 小夏: 你们都坐我的车回家吧。小王，我先 sòng 你还是先 sòng 小张？

小王: 先 sòng 我。我家_____。 (A 比 B . . .)

b. 小高: 好久不见! 你_____ 了! (漂亮, yuè 来 yuè . . .)

小Lín: 哪里，哪里。你也是。

c. 小张: 这个学期你怎么不上中文课了？

小马：Yǔ 法 yuè 来 yuè 难 ，我_____! 所以不上了。 (V不了)

d. 小谢: 你觉得我应该买哪一件衣服？

小夏: 都可以。_____ 。 (A 跟 B一样 . . .)

e. 小高: 屋子里很 mēn, 你怎么不把 chuānghù 打开？

小王: 我_____, 所以我不想开 chuānghù。 (pà . . .)

3. Making connections

Complete each sentence with the clauses below. For the first part of the sentence, make your choice from the column on the left. For the second part of the sentence, make your choice from the column on the right. Translate the sentences into English.

A. 我最喜欢 qiū 天	F. 没有时间做功课
B. 这门课很有用，也很有意思	G. 去图书馆做功课
C. 周末我常常在宿舍睡觉	H. 天 气不冷也不热，非常 shū 服
D. 昨天我跟小王一起做功课、看电 shì	I. 功课特别多
E. 我一天都忙 zhe shōushi 房间	J. 还一起吃晚饭。

a. _____, 因为天 气不冷也不热，非常shū服。

English:

b. 昨天我跟小王一起做功课、看电shì, érqiě _____

English:

c. _____, huòzhě 去图书馆做功课

English:

d. _____, 所以 _____

English:

e. _____, 只是 _____

English:

4. 天气 yùbào (Use and structure 21.2, 21.3, 21.5, 21.7, 21.8)

Part I. Six weather forecasters are presenting forecasts for their cities. Identify each forecaster based on their forecast and write each person's name into the blank space in their forecast. Then translate each forecast into English.

a. 大家好，我是_____明天的天气还是跟这几天一样，非常 shū 服。虽然有一点儿 fēng ，可是不大，是出去 玩的好天气 。

Translation:

b. 大家好，我是_____。大家可能觉得，今年的 dōng 天怎么这么长。明天特别冷 ，最 zāogāo 的是，很可能会下大 xuě，如果没有事，就在家里别出去，在路上开车的时候，最好开慢一点。

Translation:

c. 大家好，我是_____。最近这几天又 mēn 又热，我想很多人都快 shòu 不了了。明天还是很热，不过下午会下一点儿 yǔ。应该会让大家高兴一点。

Translation:

d. 大家好，我是_____。下 yǔ 下了一天了，大家今天一定觉得很不 方 biàn。明天 chú 了下 yǔ 以外，还会 guā 大 fēng 。这样的天气要到周末才会有一点不同。

Translation:

e. 大家好，我是_____明天会 比今天 冷 得多，érqiě 可能会下 xuě，出去的时候，别 wàng 了多 穿 一点衣服。

Translation:

f. 大家好，我是＿＿＿＿＿。不知道你是不是跟我一样，也觉得 chūn 天快到了。最近白天 (daytime) yuè 来 yuè 长。明天也是一个好天气,不冷不热，shū 服 jí 了 。

Translation:

Part II. It's your turn to be the weather forecaster! Check the weather forecast online or on TV, and write about tomorrow's weather in Mandarin.

＿＿＿＿＿＿＿＿＿＿＿＿＿＿＿＿＿＿＿＿＿＿＿＿＿＿

＿＿＿＿＿＿＿＿＿＿＿＿＿＿＿＿＿＿＿＿＿＿＿＿＿＿

＿＿＿＿＿＿＿＿＿＿＿＿＿＿＿＿＿＿＿＿＿＿＿＿＿＿

＿＿＿＿＿＿＿＿＿＿＿＿＿＿＿＿＿＿＿＿＿＿＿＿＿＿

＿＿＿＿＿＿＿＿＿＿＿＿＿＿＿＿＿＿＿＿＿＿＿＿＿＿

5. 一年四 jì 我最(不)喜欢 . . . (Use and structure 21.2, 21.3)

Part I. Students in 小张's class each talked about the season they like or dislike the most. Complete each sentence based on the illustrations.

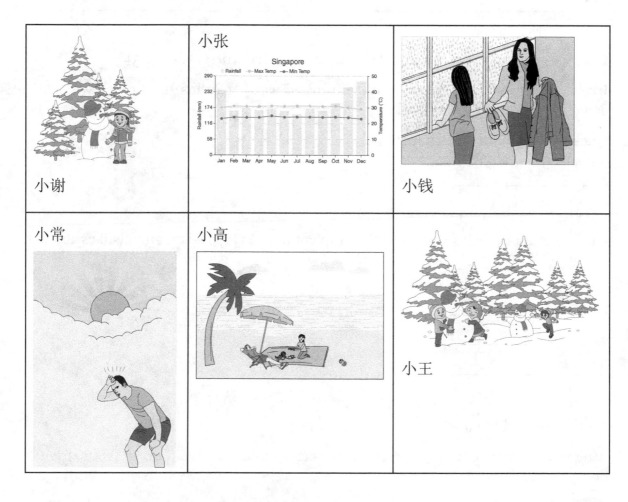

a. 小谢最不喜欢 dōng 天，因为 dōng 天＿＿＿＿＿＿＿＿＿＿＿＿＿。

b. 小张家 xiāng 的天气，一年四 jì 都＿＿＿＿＿＿＿＿＿＿＿＿＿。

c. 小钱不喜欢 qiū 天，因为 qiū 天 _____。

d. 小常最不喜欢夏天，因为夏天_____, 他 shòu 不了。

e. 小高最喜欢夏天，因为夏天_____。

f. 小王最喜欢 dōng 天，因为 dōng天_____。他可以跟朋友_____ 。

Part II. It's your turn. Tell us your (least) favorite season in your hometown and explain why.

_____

_____

_____

_____

_____

_____

_____

6.   你家 xiāng 的天气怎么样？   (Use and structure 21.2, 21.3)

Interview a friend and find out the year-round weather in his/her hometown. Write down the questions you can ask.

Questions about his/her hometown:

a. _____

b. _____

Questions about each season: length, temperature, what s/he likes and dislikes about it.

a. _____

b. _____

c. _____

d. _____

7.   Writing (Use and structure 21.2, 21.3)

After your interview, write a short passage about the weather in your friend's hometown.

_____

_____

_____

_____

_____

_____

_____

_____

8. Scrambled paragraph

Rewrite these sentences, putting them in the correct order to construct a **persuasive paragraph** about studying Chinese.

1. Dì二，中国和美国是两个很不一样的国家，在学习中文的时候你可知道一些中国文化。

2. Dì一，现在中国的经济 yuè 来 yuè 好，中国和美国的关系也很好。 很多工作都要会说中文的人。

3. 多学一些不同的文 化很有意思。

4. 选不选中文 zhuānyè 没有关系，但是你在上大学的时候最好学一些中文。 呢？

5. 这样，你会比较有兴趣，可以学得很快、当然也就可以学得很好。

6. 你会说中文， bìyè 以后就容易找工作。

7. 人少的时候，老师和学生的关系，同学和同学的关系都比较好。

8. Dì三，中文课和数学课、经济课很不一样，中文课，每个课的学生比较少。

Lesson 22 Duànliàn 身体
Working out

🎧 Listening and speaking

Listening comprehension exercises, structure drills for listening and speaking practice, audio files for vocabulary, and the sentence pyramids are on the companion website.

Focus on literacy

Additional exercises focusing on Chinese characters are on the companion website.

1. First two strokes

Consult the stroke order flow chart in the textbook and write the first **two** strokes of each of the following characters.

a. 而   f. 雪

b. 教   g. 练

c. 者   h. 队

d. 舞   i. 参

e. 或   j. 雨

2. Radicals

a. The following are characters that we have learned through this lesson. Rewrite each character in the row next to its radical.

陪	作	怕	空	队	放	快	考	累	穿
教	系	老	数	惯	者	除	忙	体	院

阝	
穴	
攵	
亻	
少	
纟	
忄	

b. How does the radical 穴 contribute to the meaning of the character 空? How does the radical 亻 contribute to the meaning of the character 体? Consult the *Focus on Radicals* file for Lesson 22 on the companion website as you do this exercise.

3. Find the bùjiàn (部件 component parts)

The following are characters introduced in this and previous lessons along with a list of **bùjiàn** (部件 *component parts*) that recur in many characters. Some of these component parts serve as the radical in the character in which they occur, and some do not. Write each character next to a component part that it includes. You may use a character more than once.

爱   百   体   最   床   变   校   想   现   友   怕   欢

末   视   练   宿   发   果   觉   趣

Shared part	Characters
又	
白	
东	
木	
见	

4. Look for the rhymes

The following is a list of characters that you have learned. Pair each character with another on the list that rhymes or nearly rhymes with it and shares a shēngpáng (声旁) "phonetic element."

For Lesson 22:

饺   院   生   女   只   较   漂   远   每   如

方   孩   里   母   房   先   校   识   选   姓

完   该   理   现   旁   票   馆   玩   放   管

Phonetic	Characters that rhyme or almost rhyme and with this phonetic component
女	
方	
只	
母	
见	
元	
先	
生	
里	
亥	
交	
官	
票	

5. Reading for basic information

We have learned all of the words, but not all of the characters, in the following passage. Complete the tasks that follow the passage and you will understand all, or almost all, of it.

快放寒假了。同学们都在计划放假的时候到哪儿去玩，好好儿地休息一下。有的同学想去南边，那边气候好、暖和，可以到海边去玩儿去游泳。有的同学想到北边冷的地方去滑冰或者去滑雪。我的室友张明问我寒假要不要跟他和另外两个同学一起去滑雪。我不知道我去不去。能滑雪的地方一定很冷。 天气冷就要穿很多衣服。穿很多衣服不舒服。如果冷得连手都伸不出来，会让人受不了。另外，除了滑雪还可以做什么呢？

a. Find and circle the following words and indicate how many times each word occurs in the passage.

同学

南边

北边

玩

b. Underline the verb phrases in which 南边 and 北边 occur. What do these phrases mean?

c. A: What is the subject of the verb phrase that includes 南边? Put a box around it.

   B: What is the subject of the verb phrase that includes 北边? Put a box around it.

d. The author lists two activities that you can do in the 南边 and two that you can do in the 北边. Place a double underline below each of these activities.

e. The author's roommate has made a suggestion. Put square brackets around the suggestion.

f. What does the author think about the roommate's suggestion? The author does not say directly, but the description s/he gives provides a lot of clues.

   A: List two things that the author says that conveys his/her opinion about the room-mate's suggestion.

   B: Where do you think the author will go? Why?

6. Dictionary skills

Following the instructions in Lesson 17 of the textbook, look up these characters in a Chinese dictionary and provide the following information:

a. 寒

   pronunciation:

   meaning:

b. 假

   pronunciation:

   meaning:

   What does 寒假 mean? _____

c. 舒

   pronunciation:

   meaning:

   What does 舒服 mean? _____

7. Proofread 大为's email

大为 has written this email to his parents back in the US telling them about how he is spending his free time during the cold Beijing winter. He hasn't yet proofread this message, but when he does, he will find that 14 different characters are wrong, one more than once. Read the passage aloud, circle the mistakes, and correct them on the answer sheet below.

巴巴妈妈你们好，

最进几天天气非长冷，可是我的同屋还想到外边去大 lán 球。我跟他说今天那么冷，lián 手也 shēn 不去来，怎么能去打球呢？他说一开室打球，pǎo bù，就不会觉的冷了。他说了半天可是我镇的不想去。最候他跟别人去打球，我一个下午都在宿舍离看电视上的 lán 球比 sài。我不是不洗欢 duànliàn，只是冬天我比教喜欢室内活 dòng，每个星期都去 jiàn 身房 duànliàn 几次。这个周末我还要帮一个朋右复习课问，zhǔnbèi 下星期的考试。

希望你们的身体 jiànkāng。

儿子，

大为

1.	2.	3.	4.	5.	6.	7.
8.	9.	10.	11.	12.	13.	14.

8. Scrambled sentences

Rewrite these phrases as sentences, putting the words in the correct order to match the English translations.

a. zhí得/的què/guān心的话题/jiéyuē/一个/能yuán/是

Conserving energy is definitely a topic worth caring about.

b. 比/qí自行车/方biàn/gèng/有的时候/开车

Sometimes riding a bike is more convenient than driving.

c. 为了/ 去/gèng /她/ yóuyǒng/让 / jiànkāng/每天/是 / 身体

The reason she goes swimming every day is to make her body stronger.

d. 以后/lìng外/身体/让 / 作 wán/会 / 你 /对 /觉得/很 / yújiā/shū服/好

Yoga is good for the body, and in addition, after you finish it makes you feel relaxed (comfortable).

9. Typing practice

Type the following sentences in Chinese characters and translate them into English. You can type the underlined words in pinyin, as we have not yet learned the characters. Be sure to proofread your typed sentences!

a. Wǒ xiǎng nǐ jīntiān yīdìng chī de bù <u>gòu.</u>

b. Měiguórén dào<u>dǐ</u> xǐhuān bù xǐhuān tī <u>zúqiú</u>?

c. Wǒ bǐ Wáng lǎoshī gāo de duō。

Focus on structure

1.   Similarities and differences (Use and structure 22.1, 22.2)

Write a sentence for each of the following lines stating that A and B have similarities and differences when it comes to C, and translate your sentence into English, as in the example.

Example:

A: 美国的大学生   B: 中国的大学生   C: **duànliàn** 身体·

美国的大学生跟中国的大学生在 **duànliàn** 身体上有 **xiāng** 同的地方，也有不同的地方。

When it comes to exercising, American students and Chinese students have similarities and differences.

a. A: 北京   B: Tái北   C: 天气

Your sentence: _____

English translation: _____

b. A: 美国   B: 中国   C: 文化

Your sentence: _____

English translation: _____

c. A: 美国大学生   B: 中国大学生   C: 学习

Your sentence: _____

English translation: _____

2.   Stating similarities (Use and structure 22.2)

Continuing the comparisons you introduced in Exercise 1 above, write a Mandarin sentence stating that *the similarity is . . .* as in the example:

Example: **Xiāng** 同的地方是 . . . 都 . . . "

a. The summer is very hot.

b. American students and Chinese students are all hard working.

c. Before college students graduate, they have to select a major.

3.   Differences and linked with 而 (Use and structure 22.2, 22.9)

Continuing the comparisons you introduced in Exercise 1 above, write a Mandarin sentence for each pair that you are comparing stating that *the differences are . . .* Link the differences with 而.

a. Beijing's summer is relatively short, and Taipei's summer is very long.

b. When they watch television, American people like to watch American football, and Chinese people like to watch soccer.

c. American students select their major when they are in their third year, and Chinese students select their major before they begin to attend college. (Use 才 in this sentence).

4.   Even more (Use and structure 22.4)

Translate (a)–(c) into English. Rewrite (d)–(f) in Mandarin.

a. 天气 yùbào 说明天比今天还冷。

b. 有人觉得 duànliàn shēntǐ 比学习还重要。

c. Qí 自行车比走路快。 开车 gèng 快。

d. Japanese is hard all right, but Chinese is even harder. (Use **gèng**.)

e. Soccer is more interesting than American football. (Use **gèng**.)

f. She is even smarter than her older sister. (Use 还.)

5.   What else do they do? (Use and structure 22.6)

Interview three classmates to find out what they do for exercise. Ask for two activities, and connect them with **ling** 外 *in addition*. Describe your classmates here:

a. _____

b. _____

c. _____

6.   Directional expressions (Use and structure 22.10, 22.11)

Write a sentence using a verb of motion with a directional complement describing the motion in each of the following pictures from Màikè's perspective. Do not include the phrases "towards Màikè" or "away from Màikè" in your sentences.

a.		ride down, towards Màikè
b.		ride up, away from Màikè
c.		jump down, towards Màikè（tiào jump）
d.		drive up, away from Màikè
e.		ride across, towards Màikè

f.		run in (into the house), towards Màikè
g.		ride out (out of the park), away from Màikè
h.		run out (out of the house), towards Màikè
i.		walk in (into the park), away from Màikè
j.		walk up (up the mountain), towards Màikè

7.   They can't do it (Use and structure 20.6, 22.11)

Rewrite each of your sentences in Exercise 6 above from Màikè's perspective, saying that the subject is unable to do the action.

a. _____

b. _____

c. _____

d. _____

e. _____

f. _____

g. _____

h. _____

i. _____

j. _____

8.   Walk out of the park (Use and structure 20.6, 22.11)

Rewrite each of your sentences in Exercise 6 above from Màikè's perspective, adding in the location that serves as the reference point of the action. (a) is completed for you as an example.

a. 他 **qí** 下山来了。

b. _____

c. _____

d. _____

e. _____

f. _____

g. _____

h. _____

i. _____

j. _____

9.   Even they can do these activities (Use and structure 22.12)

Translate (a)–(d) into English, and translate (e)–(h) into Mandarin, using characters where we have learned them. Complete (i)–(k) with the phrases provided in parentheses.

a. 自行车容易 qí。Lián 我妹妹都能 qí。

b. 我弟弟很喜欢打球。Lián pái 球也喜欢（打）。

c. 他不懂中文。Lián "你好" 也不懂。

d. 我的同屋每天都去 jiàn 身房 duànliàn 身体。 她 lián 周末都去。

e. In my hometown, it is cold in the spring. It is even very cold in April.

f. My older sister is very hard working. She even studies on Friday night.

g. In my school, a lot of students participate in school sports teams. Even the first-year students participate.

h. Yesterday's test was too long. Even the smartest students didn't finish it.

i. 大为每天都去pǎo bù, _____. (下雪的时候)

j. 国强的房间 luànjí了, _____. (坐的地方)

k. 大为昨天很不shū 服。一吃东西就 lā dù子, _____ (水)

10.   It's (good) all right, but . . . (Use and structure 22.13, 22.14)

Following the example below, say that NP$_1$ has the quality of the adjectival verb, but that it doesn't have as much as NP$_2$.

Example:

NP$_1$	NP$_2$	AdjV
movie tickets	*football game tickets*	*expensive*

电 yǐng 票贵是贵， 可是没有 zú 球比 sài 票那么贵。

Movie tickets are expensive all right, but they are not as expensive as football game tickets.

	NP₁	NP₂	AdjV
a.	huá chuán	pá山	难
b.	Hán 国 cài	四chuān cài	là

(Hán 国 *Korea*)

	NP₁	NP₂	AdjV
c.	体 yù	学习	重要
d.	qiū 天	chūn 天	漂亮

11.   Comparisons with 没有 (Use and structure 22.14)

Following the example, write a complete Mandarin sentence for each line saying that NP₁ is not as AdjV as NP₂.

Example:

NP₁	NP₂	AdjV
my hobbies	my roommate's hobbies	many

我的爱好没有我同屋的爱好那么多。

NP₁	NP₂	AdjV
a. American football	soccer	interesting
b. June	July	hot
c. my older sister	my older brother	hard working
d. taking a bus	riding a bike	convenient
e. my room	your room	messy

12.   NP₁ has a lot more of some quality than NP₂ (Use and structure 22.15)

Following the example and using the same situations as in Exercise 10 above, say that NP₂ has a lot more of the quality of the adjectival verb than NP₁. Then say that NP₃ has even more of that quality.

Example:

NP₁	NP₂	AdjV	NP₃
my hobbies	my roommate's hobbies	many	my older sister's hobbies

我同屋的爱好比我的爱好多得多。我姐姐的爱好gèng多。

NP₁	NP₂	AdjV	NP₃
a. American football	soccer	interesting	basketball
b. June	July	hot	August

c. my older sister   my older brother   hard working   my younger brother

d. taking a bus   riding a bike   convenient   driving a car

e. my room   your room   messy   my roommate's room

13. 什么意思？ (Use and structure 22.7)

Answer these questions in one or two sentences each in Mandarin. You may want to include the expressions 比方说 and 等等 in your responses.

a. "环 **bǎo**"是什么意思？

b. "室 **nèi** 活 **dòng**" 是什么意思？

c. "**shòu** 不了"是什么意思？

d. "生 **mìng** 在 **yú yùndòng**"是什么意思？

14. Where do they come from? (Use and structure 22.17)

Help these students introduce themselves and say where they come from, as in the example.

Example:

张大为: American

我姓张叫大为，来自美国。

a. 高美丽: French
b. 谢国强: China
c. 西美月: Japan
d. 王明: France

15. Scrambled sentences

Rewrite these phrases into sentences, putting them in the right order to match the English translations.

a. 做/没有/开始/忙zhe/打球/ 功课/学期/时间/学生/一 / 都/而

Once the semester begins, the students are all busy doing their course work and do not have time to play ball.

b. 喜欢/身体/ 喜欢/ duànliàn/到dǐ/你 / 不

Do you really like to work out or not?

c. 吗/了 / pǎo 上/ 你/他 / 大为/去 / 看得见/山 (2 sentences)

Dawei ran up the mountain. Can you see him?

d. 真/冷 / 下雪/可是/冷 / 漂亮/北京/是 / 的时候/dōng 天

Winter in Beijing is indeed cold, but it's really beautiful when it snows.

e. xiāng 同/在 / 和/习惯/ 她/生活/ 很不/上 / 她妹妹

When it comes to daily habits, she and her younger sister are very different.

16. Translations

Translate these sentences into English.

a. **Duànliàn** 是为了让身体 **gèng jiànkāng**。

b. **Jiéyuē** 能 **yuán** 是为了 **bǎohù** 环 **jìng** 。

c. 参加校队的学生没有空出去玩。除了参加比 **sài** 以外，他们每天都得去 **jiàn** 身房 **duànliàn**、重 **liàng xùn** 练、**pǎo bù** 等等。

d. 你可以做很多 **bǎohù** 环 **jìng** 的事情， 比方说你可以 **qí** 自行车或坐公共汽车而不开自己的车等等。

e. 花一个晚上复习功课准备明天的考试，**gòu** 不 **gòu**？

Focus on communication

Additional Focus on communication exercises as well as classroom activities for spoken communication are on the Teachers' Resource website.

1. What do you say?

What do you say in each of the following situations? **Type your answers**, using characters where we have learned them.

a. You're a volunteer at a college tour. Tell the visitors that your college has a lot of sports teams. Name a few as examples.

b. Ask someone how frequently s/he works out at the gym per week.

c. Advise your friend that s/he should exercise more.

d. Argue that your daily exercise is walking to school every day and never taking the elevator.

e. Tell people not to jump (**tiào** in **tiào wǔ**) down.

f. You are competing with your sibling/roommate/friend. Brag about two things that you do much better than s/he does.

g. You are arguing with your friend about winter in your city. You agree that he has a point (yes, it's cold) but you have a different opinion about winter.

h. You wonder whether your roommate wants to go skiing with you after all.

i. Tell your little brother running is for making yourself even healthier.

j. Tell your friend you prefer indoor sports because you are afraid of cold temperatures.

2.   Mini-dialogues (Use and structure 22.3, 22.9, 22.11, 22.12, 22.13, 22.19)

Write a sentence using the structure in the parentheses to complete each mini-dialogue.

a. A: 王老师，中文和英文最大的不同是什么？

   B: _____ 。
     (. . . 而 . . .)

b. A: 你最近在忙什么？怎么都没看见你？

   B: 我每天都忙 **zhe**_____ 。
     (**lián** . . . 都 . . .)

c. A: 你昨天说 **dù** 子 **téng**，现在呢？还 **téng** 不 **téng**？

   B: 现在好多了。_____ 。 (没有 . . . 那
     么 . . .)

d. A: 四 **chuān** 菜真好吃！

   B: _____ 。 (A 是 A, 可
     是 . . .)

e. A: 我问了你那么多次，你_____? (到 **dǐ**)

   B: 我怎么会不喜欢你呢！你想太多了。

f. A: 你最近怎么开始做 **yújiā** 了？

   B: 我开始做 **yújiā**, 是_____ 。（为了）

3.   Multiple-choice (Use and structure 22.6, 22.9, 22.12)

Select the appropriate line to complete each sentence, and then translate the sentence into English.

a. 我和我妹妹很不一样。我很喜欢走路 **duànliàn shēntǐ**, 而_____

   1. 我昨天走路走了一个钟头。

   2. 她只喜欢坐车、坐电 **tī**。

   3. 她今年是一年级的学生。

English:

b. 小美的 **shēntı** 很好，她每天 **yùndòng, lìng**外, _____

  1. 她还参加学校的跳舞队。

  2. 小美这个学期选了四门课。

  3. 小张不喜欢 **yùndòng**。

English:

c. 加 **zhōu** 漂亮是漂亮，可是_____

  1. 天 **qì** 真好。

  2. 我比 **jiào** 喜欢 **Niǔyuē**。

  3. 在加 **zhōu** 开车很方 **biàn**。

English:

d. **Yùndòng** 对 **shēntı** 很好，而 **qiě**_____

  1. 今天这么冷，我就不出去 **yùndòng** 了。

  2. 美国大学生跟中国大学生在 **yùndòng** 上有 **xiāng** 同的地方，也有不同的地方。

  3. 我觉得 **yùndòng** **wán**以后特别 **shū** 服。

  English:

e. 下雪的时候，我喜欢在家睡觉或者_____

  1. 喝一 **bēi** 热茶, 看看外边的雪

  2. 路上很 **zāng**，不能出去玩儿。

  3. 冷得手都 **shēn** 不出来。

  English:

f. 他每天早睡早起，是为了_____

  1. 他六点就起床。

  2. 让身体 **gèng jiànkāng**。

  3. **yī** 生让他早一点睡。

  English:

4. Sports schedule (Use and structure 22.8)

The following is a sports schedule at a college in California. Answer the following questions based on this schedule.

Team	Date	Opponent
Soccer	2/18	UC Irvine
Basketball	2/18	UC Davis

Team	Date	Opponent
Basketball	2/19	UC Santa Barbara
Sailing	2/22	UC Berkeley
Volleyball	3/1	CSU Long Beach
Sailing	3/2	UC Santa Cruz
Cycling	3/2	UC Davis
Cycling	3/4	Caltech
Swimming	3/5	UC Riverside
Swimming	3/9	UCLA

a. 这个学校有什么校队？

_____

b. 小周特别喜欢看 **zú** 球比 **sài**，你想他哪一天一定会去看比 **sài**？

_____

c. 二月二十二号这个学校跟哪个学校比 **sài**？比什么？

_____

d. 小王参加 学校的 **lán** 球校队，你想他哪天大概不能去上课？

_____

e. **Lán** 球比 **sài** 早还是自行车比 **sài** 早？

_____

f. 今天是二月二十八号，你觉得我还能买到 **pái** 球比 **sài** 的票吗？为什么？

_____

5.   Reading (Use and structure 22.10, 22.11)

Part I. Read the paragraph and fill in the blanks with the verb + directional complement based on the English translation.

今天是美音的生日。小张让美音下了课以后就在 **kāfēi** 馆等他 。小张_____ **(walked into the coffee shop)** 的时候，看见小谢和小高_____ **(run out)**。美音说，小谢和小高听说今天是她的生日，他们要让她高兴一下。小张让美音把手_____ **(extend out)**，他给美音买了一件漂亮的衣服。美音非常高兴。他们两个人一起_____ **(walk out of the coffee shop)**，看见小谢的车_____ **(drive over)**，小高让他们_____ **(get in/enter in)**，小谢打 **suàn** 带他们去吃晚饭。

Part II. Read the paragraph again. Imagine what was said during those situations:

a. Xiao Xie wonders what Meiyin is doing in the coffee shop and Meiyin explains.

小谢：

美音：

b. Xiao Zhang is surprised to see Xiao Xie and Xiao Gao rushing out and asks them where exactly (到**dǐ**) they are going and why they are running so fast.

_____

c. Xiao Zhang asks Meiyin to extend her hand and wishes her a happy birthday.

_____

d. Meiyin gushes about the beautiful gift and thanks Xiao Zhang.

_____

e. Xiao Gao tells Xiao Zhang and Meiyin to hurry and get into the car.

_____

6. Your favorite sports/workout (Use and structure 22.8)

Part I. Answer the following questions truthfully.

a. 你喜欢 **yùndòng** 吗？你最喜欢什么 **yùndòng?**

_____

b. 你是什么时候开始做这个 **yùndòng** 的？

_____

c. 你为什么喜欢这个 **yùndòng?**

_____

d. **Yùndòng** wán以后，你觉得怎么样？

_____

e. 这个 **yùndòng** 有什么好的地方？有没有不方 **biàn** 的地方？是什么？

_____

f. 你一个星期做几次这个 **yùndòng?**

_____

g. 你在哪儿做这个 **yùndòng?**

_____

h. 下雨或者天气不好的时候，如果你不能 **yùndòng**，你怎么 **duànliàn** 身体？

_____

i. 除了你最喜欢的这个 **yùndòng**以外，你还想试试什么 **yùndòng**，为什么？

_____

Part II. Use your answers above to write a paragraph about your favorite sports.

_____

_____

_____

_____

_____

_____

_____

_____

7.   Comparison paragraphs

Part I. The following sentences come from a paragraph that compares college life in the past with life nowadays. Rearrange the sentences so that they become a cohesive paragraph.

a. 还可以跟朋友一起出去玩，很晚才回宿舍也没有关系 。

b. 不同的是， 以前的大学生跟朋友在宿舍、**cāntīng**、咖啡馆说话，去图书馆找上课要用的书。

c. 不过很多事都得自己做，**lián** 衣服都得自己洗。

d. **Lìng** 外 ，有了电脑以后，选课、买书，都比以前方**biàn**。

e. 以前的大学生跟现在的大学生在生活上有 **xiāng** 同的地方，也有不同的地方。

f. 在学校住可以自己决定吃饭、睡觉的时间。

g. 而现在的大学生上网跟朋友说话、找上课要用的东西。

h. **Xiāng** 同的是年 **qīng** 人都喜欢住校的生活。

Part II. Following the structure of the above paragraph, write a similar paragraph to compare high school life and college life from your own experience.

_____

_____

_____

_____

_____

_____

_____

8.　环保问题

Part I. 我们应该怎么 **jiéyuē** 能 **yuán**?

(For #1–3, complete the sentences based on your own experience and knowledge.)

1. 多走路，少_____

2. 洗wán手以后要_____

3. 从房间出去的时候别忘了_____

(For #4–6, guess the underlined word and explain your answer based on your under-standing of each character in English.)

4. 看wán的 **zázhì (magazines)**，用过的 **zhǐ** 要<u>回收</u>，可以做<u>再生纸</u>。

回收：_____

再生纸：_____

5. 去咖啡馆可以<u>自备</u> **bēi**子，少用<u>**zhǐbēi**</u>。

自备：_____

Zhǐ bēi:_____

6. 少买 **xīn** 衣服，买<u>二手衣</u>。_____

Part II. Design a Chinese poster about environmental protection or measures you can take to protect the planet/conserve energy.

Part III. Read the following paragraph and decide whether the statements are true or false.

Greta Thunberg 来自 **Sweden**, 是一个十六岁的女 **hái**。 八岁的时候她第一次学到，地球 **yuè** 来 **yuè** 热， 北 **jí** 的 **bīng yuè** 来 **yuè** 少，跟全球暖化有关系。**Greta** 觉得全球暖化是一个非常 **zhí** 得关心的话题，如果大家不好好地照 **gù** 这个地球，将来，人们就没有地方可以住。所以她决定不上学了。去很多国家 **lǚ** 行，**gàosù** 大家环境的重要。她说，如果大人不关心我们的将来，我们只能自己来关心。她的话，让很多学生，都开始关心全球暖化的问题。**Time zázhì** 说，**Greta Thunberg** 是 2019 最重要的人。

_____Greta 的家在 Sweden。

_____Greta 刚学到全球暖化这个话题。

_____北 **jí** 的 **bīng yuè** 来 **yuè** 少，就是因为地球的 **wēndù yuè** 来 **yuè** 高。

_____照 **gù** 这个地球，是为了让将来的人有地方住。

_____**Greta** 不上学，因为她想 **lǚ** 行，看看别的国家。

_____**Greta**觉得大人都不关心他们的将来。

_____*Time* **zázhì** 觉得**Greta** 做的事非常重要。

Lesson 23 Guàng jiē
Going shopping

🎧 Listening and speaking

Listening comprehension exercises, structure drills for listening and speaking practice, audio files for vocabulary, and the sentence pyramids are on the companion website.

Focus on literacy

Additional exercises focusing on Chinese characters are on the companion website.

1. First two strokes

Consult the stroke order flow chart in the textbook and write the first **two** strokes of each of the following characters.

a. 颜   f. 动

b. 连   g. 铁

c. 春   h. 条

d. 简   i. 单

e. 爬   j. 短

2. Radicals

a. The following are characters that we have learned through this lesson. Rewrite each character in the row next to its radical.

虽	简	保	春	送	末	概	连
起	暖	条	管	越	便	另	运

口	
木	
走	
辶	
亻	
竹	
日	

b. How does the radical 日 contribute to the meaning of the character 暖? How does the radical 辶 contribute to the meaning of the character 运? Consult the *Focus on Radicals* file for Lesson 23 on the companion website as you do this exercise.

3. Find the bùjiàn (部件 component parts) and look for rhymes

a. The following are characters introduced in this and previous lessons along with a list of **bùjiàn** (部件 *component parts*) that recur in many characters. Some of these component parts serve as the radical in the character in which they occur, and some do not. Write each character next to a component part that it includes. You may use a character more than once.

趣 发 现 空 校 谁 友 功 饺 左 准 视 练 连 爬 最 式 把 较 爸

Shared part	Characters
东 dōng	
车 chē	
巴 bā	
工 gōng	
见 jiàn	
交 jiāo	
隹 zhuī	
又 yòu	

b. Which of the component parts serve as the rhyme or phonetic element in the character(s) in which it occurs? Support your answer by providing the pronunciation of the characters in which the component serves as the rhyme.

4. Reading for basic information

We have learned most of the words, and most of the characters, in the following passage. Complete the tasks that follow the passage and you will understand all, or almost all, of it.

我真的不知道为什么有这么多的人喜欢打球。打球到底有什么意思呢？很多人在一起，跑来、跑去。不是把球踢出去，就是把球抢过来，又脏、又热、又累。有的时候还会伤了身体，不得不去看医生。如果真的那么喜欢球，每个人自己买一个拿回家不是很好吗？

a. Circle the phrase 打球.

b. The narrator does not directly state his/her opinion of 打球, but the passage presents it clearly. Underline three sections of the paragraph that help the narrator express that opinion.

c. Explain in English how each section supports the narrator's opinion.

d. What is the narrator's suggestion in the last sentence of the paragraph? Is the narrator serious about this suggestion? Explain your answer.

5. Dictionary skills

Following the instructions in Lesson 17 of the textbook, look up these characters in a Chinese dictionary and provide the following information:

a. 踢

   pronunciation:

   meaning:

   one two-character word or phrase in which it occurs:

b. 抢

   pronunciation:

   meaning:

   one two-character word or phrase in which it occurs:

c. 伤

   pronunciation:

   meaning:

   one two-character word or phrase in which it occurs:

6.   Proofread 大为's email

大为 has written this email to his parents back in the US telling them about how he is spending his free time during the cold Beijing winter. He hasn't yet proofread this message, but when he does, he will find that 10 different characters are wrong. Read the passage aloud, circle the mistakes, and correct them on the answer sheet below.

> 爸爸，妈妈，你们好！
>
> 你们身体好吗？北京的天汽越来月冷。宿舍，叫室都很 shū 服，可是外变得多穿衣服。Guā fēng 的时候觉得更冷。我有一个同学非常怕冷。 因为怕冷，所以他很少跟我们道宿舍外边去云动。音为很小运动，所以他也很容以累。如果有人请他出去吃反，看电 yǐng，买东四，他说如果坐地铁去，他就去。如果走路去，他就不去。

1.	2.	3.	4.	5.
6.	7.	8.	9.	10.

7.   Scrambled sentences

Rewrite these phrases as sentences, putting the words in the correct order to match the English translations.

a. 以后 / 去 / 晚饭 / 男朋友 / 新 / 市中心 / 买 / 她 / 衣服 / 和 / 的 / 吃wán / 小文

   After finishing dinner, Xiao Wen and her boyfriend went downtown to buy new clothes.

b. 的 / 天气 / 春天 / 好 / shū服 / 好 / 没有 / 的 / 那么 / 夏天 / 是 / 可是

   The weather in the summer is good all right, but it is not as comfortable as the spring.

c. 都 / 打球 / 周末 / 没有 / 时间 / 我们 / 连 / 的

   We don't even have time to play ball on the weekend.

8.   Typing practice

Type the following sentences in Chinese characters and translate them into English. You can type the words in parentheses in pinyin, as we have not yet learned the characters. Be sure to proofread your typed sentences!

a. zhè (zhǒng) chángduǎn de (qún)zi jīnnián hěn liúxíng.

b. zhè jiàn yīfú yòu piányi yòu hǎo kàn, kěshì wǒ chuān bùxià.

c. nà, nǐ shìchuān yīxià zhè jiàn dà yī hào de ba.

9. Reading comprehension

Read the following paragraph and indicate whether the statements below are true (T) or false (F) based on the information in the passage.

有的人很喜欢买东西。有用的东西也买，没有用的也买。只要看见他喜欢的东西，他就非买不可。我就认识一个这样的人。他最喜欢买不同式样的衣服。虽然买了很多，但是没有时间穿。以前差不多每个周末他都出去买衣服，最近不买了。因为他买了很多，所以现在他连一点钱都没有了。他的房间虽然很大，但是连再放一件衣服的地方都没有了。他说以后有了钱，他还会买。你说这样的人有意思吗？

( ) a. The narrator's friend only likes to buy one style of clothing.

( ) b. The narrator's friend buys clothing that he doesn't wear.

( ) c. The narrator's friend can't buy any more clothing because his house isn't big enough to store more clothes.

( ) d. The narrator's friend only buys clothing if it is on sale.

( ) e. The narrator thinks that buying clothing is interesting.

Focus on structure

1. A type of (Use and structure 23.2)

Rewrite these sentences in Mandarin, using the structure NP$_1$是一种 NP$_2$.

a. Slacks are a type of clothing.

b. Basketball is a type of sport.

c. Sandals are a type of shoe.

d. Listening to music is a type of hobby.

2. I have no alternative (Use and structure 23.3)

Your roommate is wondering about your choice of action. Explain to her why this is your only option. For your replies in (c), (d), and (e), use the expression 不得不.

a. 你的同屋：你今天怎么穿这件衣服？

你说：＿＿＿＿＿＿＿＿＿＿＿＿＿＿＿＿＿＿＿＿＿＿，所以我不得不穿这 **jiàn** 衣服。

b. 你的同屋：你不是不喜欢吃中国饭吗？为什么你会去那个饭馆吃饭？

你说：＿＿＿＿＿＿＿＿＿＿＿＿＿＿＿＿＿＿＿，所以我不得不去。

c. 你的同屋：周末要不要跟我一起去看 **lán** 球比 **sài**？

你说：我不能去。＿＿＿＿＿＿＿＿＿＿＿＿＿＿＿＿＿＿＿

d. 你的同屋：天气这么冷你还要出去运动？

你说：**Yī** 生说＿＿＿＿＿＿＿＿＿＿＿＿＿，所以我＿＿＿＿＿＿＿＿＿＿＿＿

e. 你的同屋：这个 **shāng** 店东西都很贵，也不打 **zhé**。你为什么要在那儿买 **xié?**
你说：这 **shuāng xié**，别的 **shāng** 店都卖 wán 了。我 ＿＿＿＿＿＿＿

3. As long as you do this (Use and structure 23.4)

大为 is expressing his concerns to 国强. Translate each of 大为's sentences into English, and translate 国强's responses into Mandarin, using the expression 只要 . . . 就 in each of the responses.

a. 大为：我对我的 **zhuānyè** 没有兴趣了。

国强: Whether you are interested or not is not important. As long as your grades are good, it's okay.

b. 大为： 天气 **yùbào** 说明天会很冷。

国强: As long as it doesn't snow, it's okay.

c. 大为：我们的房间又 **luàn** 又脏！

国强: It doesn't matter whether it's clean or not. As long as we have a place to sleep, it's okay.

d. 大为：明天是小文的生日。你说我应该给她买什么东西？

国强: It's not important what you buy. As long as you buy her something, she will be happy.

e. 大为：我看书看得太慢了。

国强: It doesn't matter if you read slowly. As long as you <u>understand what you are reading,</u> it's okay. (*Use a resultative verb in the potential form for the underlined expression.*)

f. 大为: 走 **lóutī** 没有坐电 **tī** 那么快。另外,没有坐电 **tī** 那么方便。

国强: It doesn't matter if it's a little slower. As long as it reduces pollution, it's good.

4.   Unable to get it down (Use and structure 23.5)

Translate these sentences into English.

a. 你别再买书了，你看，书 **jià** 已经放不下了。

b. 我的车可能坐不下那么多人，如果你们也要去，就自己开车吧。

c. 今天的饺子我很喜欢，吃了很多，真的吃不下了。

5.   The more you do it (Use and structure 23.6)

Translate sentences (a)–(d) into English and (e)–(g) into Mandarin.

a. 那家店的饺子很特别，越吃越好吃。

b. 牛肉面太 **xián** 了，越吃越 **kě**，我得喝一点水。

c. 很久没有跟你一起打球，你的球越打越好了，一定常常练习吧？

d. 你到 **dǐ** 在做什么？怎么房间越收越 **luàn**？

e. Today's homework is not interesting. The more I write it, the more bored I get.

f. This kind of clothing, the more you wear it, the more comfortable (it gets).

g. Everyone should walk more often. The more you walk the healthier you get.

6.   Not even a little (Use and structure 23.7)

Answer each of the following questions in complete Mandarin sentences using the expression: 一点都**NEG** VP and translate your answers into English.

a. 你觉得这件衣服流行吗？

   Your reply in Mandarin:

   English translation:

b. 你觉得春天穿这件衣服合适吗？

   Your reply in Mandarin:

   English translation:

c. 你觉得宿舍干净不干净跟学习的分数有关系吗？

   Your reply in Mandarin:

   English translation:

d. 你对美式 **zú** 球有兴趣吗？

   Your reply in Mandarin:

   English translation:

e. 你 **pīngpāng** 球打得怎么样？

Your reply in Mandarin:

English translation:

7. Scrambled sentences

Rewrite these phrases into sentences, putting them in the right order to match the English translations.

a. 是/**gù**客/看起来/这个/年 **qīng** 人/**shāng** 店/的 / 都

It looks like the customers for this store are all young people.

b. 合适/不 / 很/可是/式样/都 / 流行/大小/一点

The size is right, but the style isn't very popular at all.

c. **jiǎnjià**/**shāng** 店/都 / **gù** 客/让 / 春节/多 / 在/东西/到了/打 **zhé**/买

When the Chinese New Year is approaching, the stores all give discounts and reduce prices to get the customers to buy more things.

d. 觉得/**huáng** 色的/绿色/我 / 的/流行/更 / 比

I think the yellow one is more stylish than the green one.

Focus on communication

Additional Focus on communication exercises as well as classroom activities for spoken communication are on the Teachers' Resource website.

1. What do you say?

What do you say in each of the following situations? Type your answers, using characters where we have learned them.

a. Talk about one foreign language that's even more difficult than Chinese.

b. Say something nice about what your friend is wearing right now. (For example, you look good in xxx color, etc.)

c. You gained a few pounds over the holiday break. Find some excuses to explain it.

d. Request a different size piece of clothing from what you are trying on. Explain why you need another one.

e. Suggest that your friend try a pair of shoes with a different color because the green shoes don't look good.

2. Mini-dialogues (Use and structure 22.4, 23.3, 23.4, 23.7, 23.12)

Use the structure in the parentheses to complete each mini-dialogue.

a. A: 你今天为什么出来买衣服？你不是最不喜欢guàng jiē吗？

   B: _____。 (不得不)

b. A: 真 zāogāo，这么多颜色，我到 dǐ 要选哪一个？

   B: _____。 (只要 . . . 就 . . .)

c. A: 那门课不是很难吗？你为什么要选？

   B: _____。 (一点儿都不 . . .)

d. A: 我穿这 条红 qún 子怎么样，还可以吗？

   B: _____。 (看起来 . . .)

e. A: 这jiàn chènshān 你穿特别好看，一定要买！

   B: 好看是好看，可是_____。 (更)

3. Multiple-choice (Use and structure 22.11, 22.18, 23.2, 23.4, 23.7, 23.11)

Choose the correct answer based on the context, and then translate each sentence into English.

a. 这么冷的天，我真不想出去,可是_____我不得不去。

   1. 天气太冷

   2. 我不怕冷

   3. 大为的球 duì 少一个人

English:

b. 我觉得一门课难一点儿没关系, 只要 _____

   1. 有用就好。

   2. 有一点 wúliào。

   3. 老师也很 yán 。

English:

c. 她最近忙 zhe 学习、考试，_____

   1. 到 dǐ 去不去晚会？

   2. 连吃饭的时间都没有。

   3. 可是真的没有时间。

English:

d. 这 jiàn 衣服颜色好，式样简单，而且 _____

    1. 一点儿都不便宜。

    2. 买一 **jiàn** 吧。

    3. 穿在你身上特别漂亮。

    English:

e. 打zhé jiǎnjià 的时候好是好，可是 _____

    1. 人太多了

    2. 我可以买到很便宜的东西

    3. 你喜欢就好。

    English:

f. 上网买衣服又快又方便，而且， _____

    1. 不能试穿。

    2. 还有很多纸**xiāng**, 不环保。

    3. 还不 必开车出去，**jiǎn** 少空气 **wūrǎn**。

    English:

4. What are your preferences?

Use the following questions as the basis for an interview with one of your classmates. Write down their answers.

a. 你最喜欢什么颜色?

b. 你常常穿什么颜色的衣服？

c. 你的 guì 子里没有什么颜色的衣服？

d. 红色让你想到什么？

e. 买衣服的时候，式样流行比较重要, 还是穿起来舒服 比较重要?

f. 什么颜色的衣服穿起来特别 shòu? 你想过吗?

g. 如果你有一个重要的面试 (face-to-face interview), 你会穿什么？

5. Shopping experience

As a customer, explain why you are hesitating about a certain item (because of size, color, price, style. . .). As a salesperson, try your best to talk your customer into making a purchase. For example:

A mini-skirt.

Customer: 这条 qún 子很好看，就是太 短了。

Salesperson: 怎么会太短？ 今年就流行 短qún, 穿在你身上 zhèng 合适。

6.   Xiaoxue's weight loss plan

Part I. Read the paragraph and select the expressions that best complete the story.

小雪最近每天＿＿(①都 ②也) 走路去上课，在学校也不＿＿ (①走 ②坐) 电 tī，都走＿＿ (①上去 ②出去)，走下来。每天晚上去jiàn身房 duànliàn 两个小时。＿＿(①除了 ②另外) 运动以外，小雪也吃得很少。两个月以后，小雪 shòu＿＿ (①得 ②了) 很多，她自己觉得很高兴，因为她现在可以穿二号的衣服了。可是她的朋友都说，小雪以前一点都＿＿ (①没 ②不) pàng，现在 shòu＿＿ (① 是② 一) shòu, 可是＿＿ (①比 ②没有) 以前那么好看了。＿＿ (①不过 ②连) 她的男朋友都觉得她看＿＿(①起来 ②出来) 太 shòu 了，＿＿ (①让 ②对) 她多吃一点。

Part II. Read the above paragraph again and decide whether the statement is true (T) or false (F). If a statement is false, explain why in the space below the statement.

( ) 小雪有时候开车，有时候走路去学校。

＿＿＿＿＿＿＿＿＿＿＿＿＿＿＿＿＿＿＿＿＿＿＿

( ) 小雪每天的运动就是去 jiàn 身房 duànliàn 两个小时，没有别的。

＿＿＿＿＿＿＿＿＿＿＿＿＿＿＿＿＿＿＿＿＿＿＿

( ) 小雪每天都运动因为她觉得自己太 pàng 了。

＿＿＿＿＿＿＿＿＿＿＿＿＿＿＿＿＿＿＿＿＿＿＿

( ) 小雪以前穿不下二号的衣服。

＿＿＿＿＿＿＿＿＿＿＿＿＿＿＿＿＿＿＿＿＿＿＿

( ) 小雪的朋友和她的男朋友都觉得她现在 shòu一点，所以比以前好看。

＿＿＿＿＿＿＿＿＿＿＿＿＿＿＿＿＿＿＿＿＿＿＿

( ) 小雪的男朋友觉得她吃得太少了。

＿＿＿＿＿＿＿＿＿＿＿＿＿＿＿＿＿＿＿＿＿＿＿

Part III. What do YOU think? 小雪的朋友都说她太 shòu 了，没有以前好看，你觉得他们这样说，对吗？为什么？

＿＿＿＿＿＿＿＿＿＿＿＿＿＿＿＿＿＿＿＿＿＿＿

＿＿＿＿＿＿＿＿＿＿＿＿＿＿＿＿＿＿＿＿＿＿＿

＿＿＿＿＿＿＿＿＿＿＿＿＿＿＿＿＿＿＿＿＿＿＿

7.   Talk about your favorite store

Part I. Answer the following questions truthfully.

a. 你喜欢去哪个 shāng 店买东西？

b. 那个 shāng 店在哪儿？你怎么去？

c. 你多久 去一次那 个 shāng 店？

d. 你去那个 shāng 店都买什么？为什么？

e. 那个 shāng 店跟别的 shāng 店有什么不同的地方？

f. 你最近是什么时候去的？你买了什么？

g. 下次你想去买什么？

Part II. Using your answers above, imagine you are recommending your favorite store to a neighbor or friend and write down what you would say below.

_____

_____

_____

_____

_____

_____

_____

_____

_____

_____

_____

_____

_____

8.   This is how I feel about shopping

Part I. Rearrange these sentences so that they form a cohesive paragraph about shopping.

a. 现在我都上网买东西。上网比去 shāng 店方便得多。

b. 想等打 zhé 的时候再买吗？打 zhé 的时候 gù 客那么多，你想要的东西，可能早就卖 wán 了。

c. 你走进一个 shāng 店去，不一定找得到你想要的东西。

d. 我最不喜欢的事就是 guàng jiē，因为 guàng jiē 真的太花时间了。

e. 我觉得，这样的 "guàng jiē" 特别shū服。

f. 你只要坐在电 nǎo 前面，就可以慢慢地找你要的颜色、大小和式样。

g. 而且，xiāng 同的东西，常常可以找到最便宜的。

h. 有时候找到了，可是颜色或者大小不合适。有的时候东西好是好，可是太贵了。

Part II. Following the structure of the paragraph above, write a similar paragraph talking about whether you like to shop online or in a brick and mortar store. Use evidence to support your point of view.

_____

_____

_____

_____

_____

_____

_____

_____

_____

_____

_____

9. 环保和买东西

In the *Focus on communication* exercises in Lesson 22 of the workbook, we learned the following vocabulary: 回收、再生纸、自备. Read the following paragraph and answer the questions.

现在去 **shāng** 店买东西，很多店都不给你 **dài** 子了，你可以花钱买一个纸 **dài**，**huòzhě** 是自备环保 **dài**。环保 **dài** 就是可以用很多次的 **dài** 子。上网买东西也越来越流行了。动动手，连 **shāng** 店都不 必 去。少开车还可以 **jiǎn** 少空气 **wūrǎn**。可是东西送来的时候都有很多纸 **xiāng**。到 **dǐ** 好不好呢？为了这个问题，我特别上网看了一下：做再生纸用的能 **yuán** 比 做 **xīn** 的纸少得多。所以，如果大家都回收纸 **xiāng**，多用再生纸，还是可以保 **hù** 我们的地球。

1. Based on the context, explain the definition of the following words:

dài 子: _____; 纸 **dài**: _____; 环保 **dài**: _____

2. Complete this graphic organizer based on your understanding of the paragraph.

去 **shāng** 店买wán东西　　→　　　1. 花钱买纸 **dài**

　　　　　　　　　　　　　　　　2. _____

上网买东西　　　　advantages　　1. _____

　　　　　　　　　　　　　　　　2. _____

　　　　　　　　disadvantage　　　_____

3. What is this author's view of cardboard boxes from online shopping? (用你自己的话说说看。)

4. 你回收纸 **xiāng** 吗？除了回收以外，纸 **xiāng** 还可以做什么？

Lesson 24 Jiǎn 价，打折
Discounts
and bargains

🎧 Listening and speaking

Listening comprehension exercises, structure drills for listening and speaking practice, audio files for vocabulary, and the sentence pyramids are on the companion website.

Focus on literacy

Additional exercises focusing on Chinese characters are on the companion website.

1. First two strokes

Consult the stroke order flow chart in the textbook and write the first **two** strokes of each of the following characters.

a. 衫   f. 鞋

b. 位   g. 务

c. 死   h. 黑

d. 饿   i. 码

e. 楼   j. 感

2. Radicals

a. The following are characters that we have learned through this lesson. Rewrite each character in the row next to its radical.

极	流	折	热	便	价	楼	衫
位	裤	员	商	扫	信	衬	汽

口	
⺍	
氵	
亻	
扌	
衤	
木	

b. For some of these characters, the radical helps to identify the meaning of the character. Circle all of the characters for which this is the case. How is the meaning of the radical in each of these characters related to meaning of the character in which it occurs? Consult the *Focus on Radicals* file for Lesson 24 on the companion website as you do this exercise.

3. Character sleuth: Look for the phonetic

Many characters include a component part that provides a clue to its pronunciation. That part is the "phonetic" or "rhyme" in the character. Group the characters below in terms of their rhymes or near rhymes by writing each character in the column on the right following its phonetic. Notice that sometimes an entire character serves as the phonetic in another character. Notice also that sometimes the phonetic only indicates a near rhyme. That is, the pronunciation of the character is very similar but not identical to the phonetic.

妈　见　远　现　气　花　爬　较　简
玩　百　式　很　间　跟　钟　码　试
种　爸　校　怕　院　汽　化　完　吗

Phonetic	Characters that rhyme or almost rhyme and share a phonetic component
化	
中	
巴	
气	
间	
交	
见	
白	
元	

Phonetic	Characters that rhyme or almost rhyme and share a phonetic component
艮	
式	
马	

4.   Reading for information I

We have learned all of the characters and words used in this paragraph. Read it several times, completing the following tasks during each successive reading.

什么样的衣服最流行，我就最不喜欢。流行的衣服很多人都有，很多人都穿，我为什么要跟他们穿一样的衣服呢？不流行没关系，只要我自己喜欢就好。我不管别人怎么想。我给我自己穿衣服，不是给别人穿衣服。另外，流行的衣服，很多人都想买，所以也就会比较贵。本来一件衣服不会那么贵，就是因为很多人都想买才会那么贵。这就是我为什么不喜欢流行的衣服。

a. Circle any characters that you do not remember. If you are stumbling over more than five characters in the passage, review the characters from this and previous lessons before continuing.

b. Identify the topic of this paragraph: what is the author writing about? Underline this topic each time it occurs in the paragraph.

c. What is the author's opinion about this topic? Double underline the words and phrases that express the author's opinion.

d. What arguments does the author give to explain this opinion?

e. What phrase does the narrator use to sum up his/her opinion? Write the phrase here.

5.   Reading for information II

Part I. Read the following note from a mother to her son, and answer the questions *in English*. We have learned almost all of the characters in the passage. The ones that we have not yet introduced are underlined.

虽然这件衣服穿在你身上很合适，但是我觉得你应该买再大一号的。第一，穿大一点的衣服，你看起来比较瘦。第二，衣服大一号，夏天穿你不觉得很热，冬天你里边还可以再穿别的衣服。第三，这件和大一号的一样贵。最后，如果你以后高了呢，大一号的还可以穿，而现在合适的就不能穿了。

a. What is the purpose of this paragraph?

b. How does the mother's opinion differ from the opinion of her son?

c. How many reasons does the mother provide to support her opinion?

d. What is the mother's final argument?

Part II. Following the instructions in Lesson 17 of the textbook, look up these characters in a Chinese dictionary and provide the following information:

a. 第
pronunciation:

- Which component of this character provides a pronunciation clue? What is the clue?

meaning:

b. 瘦

pronunciation:

meaning:

6. Proofread 美丽's email

美丽 has written this email to her parents, but she has typed 14 characters wrong. Read the passage aloud, circle the mistakes, and correct them on the answer sheet below.

昨天我和大为和我的同屋小文到市中信去 guàng 商点。因为天汽越来越冷，所以我卖了手 tào 和 ěrzhào。我也买了心的大衣和一双红色的 pí 谢。春节以前大大小小的商店都在大折，所以我买的东西都很便以。一共花了一 qiān 多块钱。大为什么都没买，只陪我们去 guàng 街，帮我们 ná 东西。到了晚上，我们是做出 zū 车会宿舍的。下车一后，我和小文现去喝咖啡，回宿舍的时后，大为说他们太俄，已经叫了外买吃 bǎo 了。

1.	2.	3.	4.	5.
6.	7.	8.	9.	10.
11.	12.	13.	14.	

7. Scrambled sentences

Rewrite these phrases as sentences, putting the words in the correct order to match the English translations.

a. 这/贵 / 我/不 / 双/一点/觉得/鞋子/都

I think this pair of shoes isn't expensive at all.

b. jiǎn 价/ 以前/都 / 商店/打折/很多 /春节

Before the spring festival, a lot of stores reduce prices and give discounts.

c. 流行/没 / 打/流行/折 / 我/买 / 只要是/不 / 关系/就

Whether or not it is stylish isn't important. As long as it's on sale, I'll buy it.

8. Typing practice

Type the following sentences in Chinese characters and translate them into English. Type the words in parenthesis in pinyin.

a. Zài Zhōngguó mǎi dōngxi sǎo èr(wéi)mǎ zuì fāngbiàn.

b. Nǐ zhǐ kěyǐ yòng (Wéi)xīn (Zhīfù), xiànjīn méi yǒu yòng.

c. Nǐ juéde wán shǒujī (làng)fèi shíjiān ma?

Focus on structure

1. Anyone, anywhere, any time (Use and structure 24.1)

大为 is a talented, agreeable person. Here are sentences that describe him. Translate (a)–(d) into English and (e)–(g) into Mandarin, using the phrases in parentheses in your translations.

a. 谁都喜欢他。

b. 他觉得什么电 **yǐng** 都很有意思。

c. 他什么歌都能唱。

d. 他比谁都 **pǎo** 得快。

e. He understands everything. (什么)

f. He likes to go everywhere. (哪儿)

g. He helps everyone. (谁)

2. No one, nowhere, never (Use and structure 24.1)

美丽 was feeling sick yesterday. Here is how she described her day. Translate (a)–(c) into English, and (d)–(f) into Mandarin, using the phrases in parentheses in your translations.

a. 我什么东西都没吃。

b. 我谁都没看。

c. 我哪儿都没去。

d. I didn't do any homework. (什么)

e. I didn't watch any television. (什么)

f. I didn't read any books. (什么)

3.   On sale! (Use and structure 24.2)

Indicate these discounts as percentage off the price.

a. 打三折

b. 打4.5折

c. 打九折

d. 打四折

4.   Do it again! (Use and structure 24.3)

Translate these sentences into Mandarin, using 再 ActV or 又 ActV 了 *again* as appropriate.

a. This dish was delicious. Let's make it again tomorrow.

b. I've forgotten her name again. How embarrassing!

c. It's raining again. Let's stay home and watch a movie.

d. The prices in that store are really low. I'm definitely going to shop there again.

e. Don't wear those slacks again. They are too old.

f. He accompanied his girlfriend shopping again.

5.   So Adj Verb that . . . Part I (Use and structure 24.5, 24.11)

Translate the comments of these students into English.

a. **Màikè**：我最近忙得连早饭都没有时间吃。

b. 小文：学校附近的店贵死了，他们的衣服贵得谁也买不了。

c. 美丽：我昨天累得连手机都忘了开。

d. 大为：昨天我在学生 **cāntīng** 吃了一个牛 **ròu** 面，**xián** 得我一直喝水。

e. 国强：这几天冷得连穿两双袜子都不**gòu**。

6. So Adj Verb that . . . Part II (Use and structure 24.1, 24.5, 24.11)

Translate these sentences into Mandarin.

a. The test was so difficult that no one could finish it. (谁)

b. Those shoes are so stylish that everyone wants to buy a pair. (谁)

c. My hands are so cold that they are numb.

d. The book was so long that I couldn't finish reading it.

e. There were so many people that I couldn't find him. (Hint: *The people were so numerous that . . .*)

7. Not only . . . but also (Use and structure 24.6)

The following is a list of nouns and descriptions. Rewrite each line in a complete Mandarin sentence saying that the noun is *not only A but also B*, using 不但 VP₁/S 而且VP₂/S as in the example.

Example:

my younger sister: smart, hardworking

我的妹妹不但 **cōng** 明而且很用功。

a. this skirt: stylish, cheap

b. leather shoes: comfortable, nice looking

c. climbing stairs: is a type of workout, can save energy

d. this fitness center: convenient, clean

e. today's weather: cold, will snow

8. What are they wearing? (Use and structure 24.7)

Translate these descriptions into Mandarin in complete sentences, using characters where we have learned them.

a. Meili is wearing a new red skirt.

b. Guoqiang is wearing his old black slacks.

c. Dawei is wearing a pair of white gym shoes.

d. Xiaowen is wearing a blue coat and a pair of cute blue earmuffs.

e. Maike is wearing a stylish yellow shirt.

f. Meili is wearing a gold scarf.

9.   Take it (Use and structure 24.8)

大为 and 国强 are cleaning up their room again. Translate each of 国强's directions into Mandarin, using the words in parentheses.

a. Put all of the sneakers under the bed. (把, 放)

b. Bring that pair of slacks over to me. (把, **ná**, 我这儿)

c. Take all of those books back to the library. (把, **ná**)

d. Take the dirty socks into the bathroom and wash them clean. (把, **ná**, 洗干净)

e. Bring all of the basketballs and soccer balls inside and put them in the closet. (把, **ná**, 放)

10.   If it isn't one thing, it's the other thing (Use and structure 24.10)

美丽 is very predictable. These sentences describe her behavior. Translate (a)–(b) into English and (c)–(e) into Mandarin, using characters where we have learned them.

a. 美丽每天不是喝咖啡就是喝茶。

b. 美丽每天不是穿红色的裙子就是穿红色的衬衫。

c. When Meili goes to school, if she doesn't take the bus she takes the subway.

d. After Meili gets out of class, she either phones her mother or phones her older sister.

e. On the weekends, Meili and her friends either go window shopping or go see a movie.

11. Scrambled sentences

Rewrite these phrases into sentences, putting them in the right order to match the English translations.

a. 衬衫/ 这/那 / 跟/huáng色/裙子/pèi/条 / 的/件 / 很

   This skirt really matches that yellow blouse.

b. 不/家 / 的/价钱/商店/贵 / 那/本来/太

   The prices in that store were not too expensive to begin with.

c. 便宜/算 / 就/的 / 是/一点/意思/打折

   "Give a discount" means "figure the price a little cheaper."

d. 会/位 / 那/tǎo 价还价/ 小姐/真

   That young lady certainly knows how to bargain.

e. 热/天气/家xiāng/不是/冷 / 非常/的 / shū服/我 / 不/太 / 太/就是

   The weather in my hometown is either too hot or it's too cold; it's extremely uncomfortable.

Focus on communication

> Additional Focus on communication exercises as well as classroom activities for spoken communication are on the Teachers' Resource website.

1. What do you say? (Use and structure 24.2, 24.3, 24.5, 24.8)

What do you say in each of the following situations? Type your answers, using characters where we have learned them.

a. Ask the salesperson to bring you that black shirt.

b. The pair of sneakers you want is $78. Ask for a discount and provide an incentive to the salesperson. (You'll buy a second one, you'll come back, etc.)

c. Agree to give the customer a discount but ask them to keep it quiet.

d. Ask your roommate to order delivery on his cell phone.

e. Call your little brother out because you caught him watching TV again!

f. Comment on how well the skirt matches the blouse that your friend is wearing right now.

g. Tell the customer that he can pay by scanning the code here.

h. Explain to your friend that you are so tired that you don't feel like eating at all.

i. Persuade your friend to purchase the brown earmuffs because you've never seen any earmuffs cuter than this pair.

2. Mini-dialogues (Use and structure 24.1, 24.5, 24.6, 24.10)

Use the structures in parentheses to complete the mini-dialogue.

a. A: 春jià快到了，你打算做什么？

   B: 还不知道呢。我想，＿＿＿＿＿＿＿＿＿＿＿＿。 (不是 … 就是 …)

b. A: 你看这件大衣怎么样？我还没决定我到 dǐ 要不要买。

   B: 这件大衣＿＿＿＿＿＿＿＿＿＿＿＿，你一定要买。(不但 …
   而且 …)

c. A: 你来北京三个月了，去过什么地方？

   B: 我每天都忙 zhe 学习，＿＿＿＿＿＿＿＿＿＿＿。 (Question phrase 都
   NEG VP)

d. A: 我今天没时间吃中饭，＿＿＿＿＿＿＿＿＿＿＿! (AdjV 得 VP)

   B: 这儿有一些 bǐng 干，先吃一点，我现在就去做晚饭。

3. Multiple-choice (Use and structure 23.12, 24.1, 24.5, 24.6)

Using the context as your guide, choose the correct expression to complete each sentence and then translate the sentence into English.

a. 我＿＿＿＿＿＿只想去中国 lǚyóu, 可是太喜欢那儿，所以决定在那儿找工作。

   1. 因为
   2. 本来
   3. 不但

   English:

b. 你 _____很累，昨天晚上没有睡好吗？

   1. 看起来

   2. 看

   3. 觉得

   English:

c. 我家xiāng的冬天，不但很少下雪而且_____

   1. 每天都下雨。

   2. 冷得没有感觉。

   3. 比很多地方都暖和多了。

   English:

d. 我从昨天晚上开始头 téng, téng得_____

   1. 我病了。

   2. 大概是因为太冷了。

   3. 我什么都做不了。

   English:

4.   Reading comprehension (Use and structure 24.2)

Look at the following two sale flyers and answer the questions in English.

A.

大减价 SALE	冬季服饰 3 折起

a. What do you think "3折起" means?

b. What season does this sale occur in?

B.

大减价 10 元 任选 1 件	大减价 15 元 任选 2 件

This promotion is about a discount. How does the discount work?

5.   Sale promotions (Use and structure 24.2)

Match each sale promotion sign with its description below, writing the letter of the description above the matching sign. The descriptions include a few words that we have not yet learned, but that should not affect your comprehension of the main points in each description.

A. _____   B. _____   C. _____

Buy One Get One **FREE**!	Spend $50 **get $20** Now through December 3rd	Now through Sunday! Buy any regular priced item & take **50% off** any second regular priced item

D. _____   E. _____   F. _____

20% OFF when purchasing 3 or more items	4 DAYS ONLY TAKE AN EXTRA **30% OFF** ALL SALE ITEMS	WINTER CLEARANCE **SALE** Up to **70% OFF**

a. 只有四天！已经打折的东西再打七折。

b. 买一送一。

c. 从现在开始到星期天，买一件，第二件就打五折。

d. 买三件以上就打八折。

e. 冬季大jiǎn价：三折起。

f. 现在起到十二月三号，你每花五十块我们就送你二十块。

6.   Tǎo 价还价 (Use and structure 24.2, 24.7)

Imagine you're the customer. Bargain with the salesperson to get it at a lower price using the hint at the end.

a. 服务员：这条裤子是今年最流行的，只要六十四块。

Gù 客: _____ (Ask the salesperson to run it down to $60.)

b. 服务员：这 fù 手 tào 在我们这儿卖得 特别好，跟你的大衣颜色很 pèi。

Gù 客: _____ 。(Find fault in the gloves and ask for $10 off.)

c. 服务员：如果你要买这件，我可以给你打八折。

Gù 客: _____? (Offer to buy two to get a larger discount.)

d. 服务员： 七十块真的不贵, 因为这件毛衣 pèi 裙子或者裤子都好看, 什么时候都可以穿。

Gù 客: _____ 。(Ask the salesperson to take 20% off.)

7. Writing about the shopping experience

Part I. Form a cohesive paragraph. Rearrange these sentences so that they form a cohesive paragraph that explains how to be a smart shopper. (谢春美 is a person's name.)

a. 除了常常 guàng 街，<u>春美</u>也会看商店送来的电子 yóu 件和 guǎng告，就知道什么时候打折。

b. 或者，她会shēn请那家店的信用 kǎ 或会员卡_(membership card)，这样，常常有更多打折的机会。

c. 我的朋友<u>谢春美</u>跟每一个女hái子一样，很喜欢 guàng 街买衣服。 她觉得， guàng 街不一定每次都要买到东西。

d. 我觉得，春美应该当一个 YouTuber，教大家怎么用最少的钱，买到最多喜欢的衣服！

e. 有的时候虽然不买，看看商店卖的新衣服，可以知道今年流行什么，自己在家穿衣服的时候就知道怎么 pèi 比较好看。

f. 如果 guàng 街的時候看见不错的衣服，可是价钱不合适，也可以回家上网看看，常常可以找到式样差不多，价钱更便宜的。

Part II. Follow the format above, write a paragraph sharing your own shopping strategies (doesn't have to be about shopping for clothes!) or a successful one-time experience (for example, how did you get the most sought-after video game console online, etc.?).

_____

_____

_____

_____

_____

_____

8. 什么是 Wēi 信 zhīfù

What is WeChat Pay? How and where do you use it? Find out all about this digital wallet (电子钱 **bāo**) by interviewing someone you know from China (or someone who has lived in China recently), for example, a teacher, a TA, or a friend.

Part I. Translate these questions into Mandarin.

1. Have you ever used WeChat Pay? Where can you use it?

2. How do you pay with WeChat Pay?

3. Do you like it? Why?

4. Have you used it in the US (or the area in which you currently live)?

5. Besides WeChat Pay, is there another digital wallet?

6. (List another one or two questions that you want to ask):

Part II. Interview a friend and jot down the answers in Mandarin.

1. _____

2. _____

3. _____

4. _____

5. _____

6. _____

Share your answers with your classmates in class. See if they have discovered other interesting information about WeChat Pay that you are not aware of.

Lesson 25 过春节
Celebrating the New Year festival

🎧 Listening and speaking

Listening comprehension exercises, structure drills for listening and speaking practice, audio files for vocabulary, and the sentence pyramids are on the companion website.

Focus on literacy

Additional exercises focusing on Chinese characters are on the companion website.

1. First strokes

Consult the stroke order flow chart in the textbook and write the first **two** strokes of each of the following characters.

a.	蓝	f.	孩
b.	划	g.	黄
c.	鱼	h.	绍
d.	正	i.	夜
e.	龙	j.	乐

2. Radicals

a. The following are characters that we have learned through this lesson. Rewrite each character in the row next to its radical.

饱	眼	保	花	体	划	位	到
介	着	蓝	贴	假	饿	晴	贵

目	
艹	
亻	
忄	
贝	
人	
刂	

b. For some of these characters, the radical helps to identify the meaning of the character. Circle all of the characters for which this is the case. How is the meaning of the radical in each of these characters related to meaning of the character in which it occurs? Consult the *Focus on Radicals* file for Lesson 25 on the companion website as you do this exercise.

3.   Character sleuth: Look for the phonetic

Many characters include a component part that provides a clue to its pronunciation. That part is the "phonetic" or "rhyme" in the character. Group the characters below in terms of their rhymes or near rhymes by writing each character in the column on the right following its phonetic. Notice that sometimes an entire character serves as the phonetic in another character. Notice also that sometimes the phonetic only indicates a near rhyme. That is, the pronunciation of the character is very similar to but not identical with the phonetic.

孩　管　睛　饺　饱　爬　汽　且　把

吧　介　爸　饿　姐　间　式　包　价

我　气　简　试　校　请　较　馆　该

Phonetic	Characters that rhyme or almost rhyme and share a phonetic component
亥	
青	
巴	
气	
间	
交	
包	
官	
我	
且	
式	
介	

4. Proofread 大为's paragraph

Zhang Dawei is preparing a paragraph for class tomorrow. His ideas are all set but he has typed 12 characters incorrectly, several of them more than once. Read the passage aloud, circle the mistakes, and correct them on the answer sheet below.

我给你们价绍一下我的好朋友。他行黄叫建民。他是中国人，可是他在美国一经生活了十多年了，所以他的英文夜说得很好。他没年下天都跟父母会中国看 yéye、nǎinai。 我和建民茶不多每天中午都一起吃五饭、和咖啡。和咖啡的时候我们喜欢用中文liáo天，所以我的中文月来月好。

1.	2.	3.	4.	5.	6.
7.	8.	9.	10	11.	12.

5. Reading for information I

We have learned almost all of the characters and words used in the following paragraph. Read it several times, completing the following tasks during each successive reading. If you are stumbling over more than five characters in the passage, you need to review the characters from this and previous lessons before you work on the questions.

小孩子都非常喜欢过年。过年的时候可以吃很多好吃的东西，穿新衣服，跟别的小朋友一起放 biānpào，还会拿到很多红包。红包就是红颜色的信封。信封里边是钱。过年的时候，除了父母会给孩子们红包，家里来的叔叔阿姨也会给。在短短的几天里，有的小孩子可以拿到很多钱，所以他们都特别喜欢过年。他们觉得过年是他们一年里最高兴的日子。

a. What two-character word is the topic of this paragraph? Why do you say that? (Answer in Mandarin.)

b. The narrator mentions a number of reasons why children like this topic. How many does she mention? Circle them or list them here. (Answer in Mandarin.)

c. Which reason do you think is most important to the narrator? Why do you think that? (Answer in Mandarin or English.)

d. The narrator says: "红包就是红颜色的信封。" We have not learned this word 信封, but the narrator provides at least one clue about what it is. What is the clue? What do you think a 信封 is? (Answer in Mandarin or English.)

6.   Reading for information II

We have learned most of the words and characters in this passage. Read it and complete the following tasks.

一说到过春节就会说到 "年" 和 "夕" (xī *sunset, evening, dusk*) 的故事。我也上网去看了看，我看到两个完全不同的说法。一个说　　"年"　　是一个怪兽　　(guàishòu *monster*)，"夕" 除掉 (chúdiào *get rid of*) 了年。另一个说法是 "夕" 是怪兽，"年" 除掉了夕。哪个说法是对的呢？现在我们来看看过春节的说法。过春节也叫过年。大人和小孩都喜欢过年，家人跟亲戚朋友在一起做饭、聊天、包饺子。春节的前一天叫除夕。前边刚刚说了 "除" 是除掉 (chúdiào *get rid of*) 的意思。先要除掉 "夕" 人们才可以高高兴兴地过年。现在你知道哪个说法是对的了吧。

a. Underline the expression 说法 each time it occurs in the passage. How many times does it occur?

说法 is a word made up of two characters we have already learned: 说 and 法. Based on the meaning of the sentences in which 说法 occurs, what do you think 说法 means? You can check your guess when you look up the character 法 in Exercise 7 below.

b. The author provides a synonym for 过春节. What is it? Circle the passage in the text where that answer is provided.

c. How many activities does the passage indicate that are associated with the Chinese New Year? Put a box around each activity.

d. What is the relationship between 除夕 and 春节? Put a double underline under the part of the text that provides this answer.

e. According to the author, what do people have to do in order to be able to make the transition to the new year? Indicate the line number in the text where this answer is provided. _____

Is this action easy to do? There is a word in this line that provides the answer to this question. Write that word here: _____.

7.   Dictionary skills

Following the instructions in Lesson 17 of the textbook, look up these words in a Chinese dictionary and provide the following information:

a. 亲戚

   pronunciation:

   meaning:

b. 法

   pronunciation:

   meaning:

c. 聊天

pronunciation:

meaning:

8. Scrambled sentences

Rewrite these phrases as sentences, putting the words in the correct order to match the English translations.

a. 家/放假/叔叔/一 / 就/春节/计划/我 / 过 /去

As soon as vacation begins, I plan to go to uncle's house to spend Chinese New Year.

b. 「春」/你 / 贴dào了/怎么/字 / 把

Why did you hang the character "spring" upside down?

c. 他们/红包/都 / 春节/会 / 知道/拿到/ 孩子/到了

Children all know that when the spring festival comes, they will receive red envelopes.

9. Typing practice

Type the following sentences in Chinese characters and translate them into English. Type the word in parentheses in pinyin.

a. Wǒ zhèng yào gěi nǐmen liǎng wèi jièshao jièshao, nǐ zěnme jiù zǒu le?

b. Wǒ cónglái méi kànguò (lóng).

c. Tāmen zuò le yī tiān de chē, yīdiǎn dōngxi dōu méi chī.

Focus on structure

1. AdjV 不得了 (Use and structure 25.1)

Describe each of these people or objects in complete sentences using **AdjV** 不得了.

a.	(extremely tall)
小王	

b.	小马	(extremely tired)
c.	Chén 先生	(extremely busy)
d.	120 mph	(extremely fast)
e.	$$$$	(extremely expensive)

2.   What can you do lying down? (Use and structure 25.3)

Here are things that Dawei likes to do lying down, sitting, and standing. Write a sentence stating each situation using V着 in each sentence.

Lying down

a. read   →

b. listen to music   →

c. watch television   →

Standing up

d. sing   →

e. make phone calls   →

Sitting down

f. sleep   →

g. drink coffee   →

3. Don't do these while wearing your pajamas! (Use and structure 25.3)

Here are some things that you should not do while wearing your pajamas. Translate them into English, and then add two more of your own (in Mandarin).

a. 别穿着睡衣买东西。   →

b. 别穿着睡衣上课。   →

c. _____

d. _____

4. How long did she do these activities? (Use and structure 22.11, 25.5)

Part I. The following is a list of things that Meili did yesterday and the amount of time she spent on each of them. Write a complete sentence in Mandarin for each activity using the structure <u>V+O V+duration</u> as in the example.

Example: slept for seven hours: 她睡觉睡了七个钟头。

a. made dumplings (one hour)

b. used the internet (one and a half hours)

c. went shopping (half hour)

d. cleaned up her room (45 minutes)

Part II. Here are some other things that Meili did yesterday. Write a complete sentence in Chinese for each activity using the structure <u>V duration 的 O</u>, as in the example.

Example: slept for seven hours: 她睡了七个钟头的觉。

a. drove for an hour

b. did homework for an evening

c. listened to music for an afternoon

d. participated in a (swimming/rowing?) competition for a weekend

5. Multi-tasking (Use and structure 25.6)

Describe what the people are doing in each of the following pictures in complete sentences, using the structure "一边 . . . 一边 . . ."

Example:

他一边洗 zǎo 一边唱歌。

a. 张友蓝

b. 王刚

c. 谢子真

d. 常学音

e. 高大南

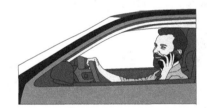

f. 钱家明和她的朋友

a. _____

b. _____

c. _____

d. _____

e. _____

f. _____

6. Never did it, never do it (Use and structure 25.10)

Màikè has invited his roommate home to Xi'an for the New Year and is going over some of the things that they will do. He wants to know if his roommate has ever done these things before. Help him ask these questions by translating them into Mandarin. His roommate has never done any of these things before. Provide his answers here, using 从来 + negation in each of his replies.

a. Have you been to Xi'an before?

   Q:

   A:

b. Have you ever seen a red envelope before?

   Q:

   A:

c. Have you set off fireworks before?

   Q:

   A:

d. Have you made dumplings before?

   Q:

   A:

7. Translation into English

Translate these sentences into English.

a. 刚才来找你的那个人是谁？

b. 真没想到用中文跟中国人 liáo 天这么容易。

c. 我刚学包饺子，所以包得不好。

d. 在床上 tǎng 着看书是非常不好的习惯。

e. 你怎么连 kuài 子都不会用。你从来没吃过中国饭吧。

f. 因为你刚学会开车，所以你一定不可以一边开车一边打电话。

g. 我的同屋每天晚上都复习好几个钟头的中文，常常一直复习到半夜。

h. 美丽把她刚买的东西拿出来给小文看。

8. Translations into Mandarin

Translate these sentences into Mandarin, using characters where we have learned them.

a. Yesterday's test was unbelievably difficult.

b. What is that noise outside? Can you hear it?

c. I have never set off fireworks before.

d. I didn't expect that the Spring Festival would be this lively.

e. I found the book that you were just looking for. It was under the bed.

f. Did you say you were born in the year of the dragon? No wonder you are so hard working!

g. I just got home and I'm dead tired. Help me prepare dinner.

h. I ate until I was full. (Use 吃 and a resultative ending.) I never expected that at midnight we would begin eating dumplings.

9. Scrambled sentences

Rewrite these phrases into sentences, putting them in the right order to match the English translations.

a. 喝/一瓶/他 / 回家/pí酒/走/拿着/一边/ 一边

Holding a bottle of beer, he drank and walked home.

b. 穿/出去/先 / 你/等到/大衣/再 / 拿着/ 的時候

Take your coat. Put it on when we go out.

c. 包/包 / 我/好 / 你/饺子/ 这么/没想到/得

I didn't know that you could wrap dumplings so well.

d. 的时候/放 / 孩子/ pǎo/看 / 剛才 / biānpào/出来/ 都

Just before when you were setting off the fireworks, the children all ran outside to watch.

e. 火車/我 / 人/坐 / 会/这么/多 / 没想到/回家/春节/的/都/有

I had no idea that there would be this many people taking the train home for the Spring Festival.

Focus on communication

Additional Focus on communication exercises as well as classroom activities for spoken communication are on the Teachers' Resource website.

1.　What do you say?

What do you say in each of the following situations? Type your answers, using characters where we have learned them.

a. You want to find out your friend's Chinese zodiac sign.

b. You want to greet people during the Chinese New Year holidays.

c. You want to know what the red envelope that parents give their kids represents.

d. You want to learn about your friend's breakfast ritual: does s/he eat standing (by the table), or sitting down?

e. You want to tell your little cousin that he has to wait until the happy birthday song ends before he eats the *cake* (dàngāo).

f. You praise your little brother that he's getting better and better at making dumplings.

g. You want to apologize to your friend that you didn't answer the phone when he called, and explain that you didn't pick up the phone because you were in the shower just a moment ago.

h. You want to complain about the movie that you just saw. You want to say that it's the worst movie you've ever seen.

i. You want to express your surprise about the subway and say that you did not expect the subway to be this crowded.

2.　Mini-dialogues (Use and structure 25.1, 25.5, 25.6, 25.7, 25.8, 25.10

Use the structure in the parentheses to complete each mini-dialogue.

a. A: 你每天吃饭的时候看电视吗？

　 B: 对，＿＿＿＿＿＿＿＿＿＿＿＿＿＿＿＿＿＿＿＿＿＿。(一边 . . . 一边 . . .)

b. A: 你知道 "好年春" 这个饭馆吗？

　 B: 对不起，＿＿＿＿＿＿＿＿＿＿＿＿＿＿＿＿＿＿＿。(从来 + negation Verb . . .)

c. A: 我妈妈包的饺子怎么样？ 好吃吗？

　 B: ＿＿＿＿＿＿＿＿＿＿＿＿＿＿＿＿＿＿＿＿＿＿＿。(AV 得不得了)

d. A: 妈妈，我什么时候才能买那双蓝色的 pí 鞋？

　 B: ＿＿＿＿＿＿＿＿＿＿＿＿＿＿＿＿＿＿＿＿＿＿。(等到 . . .)

e. A: 你看起来很累，是不是昨天晚上睡得太少？

　 B: 是 ＿＿＿＿＿＿＿＿＿＿＿＿＿＿＿＿＿＿＿＿。(V + duration 的 Obj.)

f. A: 对不起，我刚下课，所以晚了几分钟。电 yǐng 开始多久了？

B: 没问tí, _____。(刚刚)

3. 同音字

You have learned how 同音字 can carry symbolic significance in Chinese. Read the following sentences and choose the best answer. Then translate the sentence into English.

a. 过年的时候，除了吃饺子以外，中国人也喜欢吃"发菜" (literally "hair weed"), 因为吃发菜就是说你会_____ 。

I. 吃很多饭

2. 发 **cái**

3. 有长头发

English: _____

b. "sòng zhōng" 的意思就是 "陪着快要死了的父母。" 所以中国人过生日的时候最不喜欢 sòng 别人_____。

I. **zhuō**子

2. 钟 **(clock)**

3. 床

English: _____

c. 在中国，很多yī 院没有四楼 (4th floor), 因为，"四"的 shēng 音跟_____差不多。

I. "冷死了"的"死"

2. "有事"的"事"

3. "认识"的"识"

English: _____

4. Describe the pictures (Use and structure 25.3, 25.6)

Look at the following pictures and write a few sentences to describe each situation.

a. Use V着 in your sentence to describe the audience.

_____

_____

_____

_____

_____

b. Use 一边 . . . 一边 . . . in your sentence.

马大明

_____

_____

c. Use V着 in your sentence.

_____

_____

_____

_____

5.   Chinese New Year celebration

Match each picture with its description by writing the letter for the description in the line above the appropriate picture.

a. _____

b. _____

c. _____

d. _____

e. _____

f. _____

A. 包饺子，等到半夜再吃。

B. 到外边去放 biānpào。

C. 全家人在一起吃 fēngfù 的年夜饭，一边吃饭，一边liáo天。

D. 把家里收shi 干净。

E. 门上的春"字 dào 着贴。不是贴得不对，是"春到了"。

F. 小孩子最高兴的，就是可以拿到红包。

6. 我最喜欢过春节 (Use and structure 25.2)

Part I. The following paragraph talks about traditions of Chinese New Year celebration. Fill in the blanks with the letters of the sentences from Exercise 5.

一年里我最喜欢的就是春节，因为不但有好吃的，而且有好玩的。中国新年不是在一月就是在二月。每年春节，在别的地方工作、学习的人都一定会回到自己的家xiāng过节。所以那时候的火车票特别难买。春节的前几天，我妈妈就 _____，等着大姐回来过节。而爸爸忙着写春 **lián** (spring couplets, matching lines of poetry hung on either side of the door)，贴在门上。小时候爸爸就告诉我，我家_____。

除xī的早上，我们就开始做饭，晚上_____，是我最快乐的时候。晚饭以后我和大姐帮妈妈_____。包好饺子爸爸就 **dài** 着我们_____。半夜一到除了吃饺子以外，_____。因为我们可以拿着爸爸妈妈给我们的红包，去买自己喜欢的东西。第二天早上是新年，我们不是一家人开车出去玩，就是去看朋友。每个人一看到朋友就说：Gōng 喜发 cái, 新年快乐！过年那几天，每天我都高兴得不得了。

Part II. Complete the following table in Mandarin. In Column A, provide your answers based on the information in the passage in Part I. In Column B, provide information about your favorite holiday. Here are the names of two holidays in Chinese that you might want to write about:

Gǎn ēn 节 *Thanksgiving,* **Shèngdàn** 节 *Christmas.*

	Column A: 中国新年	Column B: Your favorite holiday
Time		
Significance		
Preparation		
Things that people do		
Favorite part of this holiday as a child		
Why it's my favorite holiday		

7. What is your favorite holiday?

Following the structure of the paragraph in Part I and using the information you wrote in Part II, write a paragraph talking about your fondest memories of your favorite holiday.

_____

_____

_____

_____

_____